The *Politics* of Abortion

Anne Hendershott

ENCOUNTER BOOKS
NEW YORK

First edition published in 2006 by Encounter Books, an activity of Encounter for Culture and Education, Inc., a nonprofit, tax exempt corporation.

Encounter Books website address: www.encounterbooks.com

Manufactured in the United States and printed on acid-free paper.

The paper used in this publication meets the minimum requirements of ANSI/NISOZ39.48-1992 (R 1997)(*Permanence of Paper*).

FIRST EDITION

Library of Congress Cataloging-in-Publication Data

Hendershott, Anne
      The Politics of Abortion/Anne Hendershott
         p. cm.
      ISBN 1-59403-148-7
1. Medical Policy. 2. Abortion—Political Aspects. 3. Abortion-Law and Legislation. 1. Title.

RA395.A3H462 2006
363.46—dc22
2006020660

10 9 8 7 6 5 4 3 2 1

CONTENTS

Introduction	1
CHAPTER 1	9
Looking for the Life of the Party	
CHAPTER 2	31
Race and the Politics of Abortion	
CHAPTER 3	45
Inside Abortion inside Washington	
CHAPTER 4	59
The Personal Is Political	
CHAPTER 5	77
The Politics of Celebration	
CHAPTER 6	85
Sacred Choices	
CHAPTER 7	95
Catholics and the Politics of Abortion	
CHAPTER 8	109
Campus Politics of Abortion	
CHAPTER 9	121
Signs of Life	
CHAPTER 10	135
Ending the Abortion Wars	
Acknowledgments	149
Notes	151
Index	167

INTRODUCTION

I F EVERY LAW tells a story about a society, then studying our laws should tell the story of who we are and what we believe. In the best of worlds, our laws would contain a moral story that proclaims the ideals and principles of the people who live by them. Our laws would convey our understanding of the common good and represent our willingness to work toward the good life for everyone.[1] But in the real world, we must acknowledge that many of our most important laws do not necessarily reflect the values and beliefs of a majority of the people, and instead reveal the will of those with the power to shape the laws.

Today, more than thirty years after the 1973 Supreme Court decision in *Roe v. Wade,* there are no laws that tell a more compelling or more contradictory story. For the pro-choice side, abortion laws express fundamental beliefs about life and liberty for women. For the pro-life side, on the other hand, these same laws tell a tragic story of the failure of our democratic institutions to protect the lives of the unborn. For the critics of the Court, the ruling in *Roe v. Wade* reflects the politics and the personal views of the justices rather than a careful reading of the Constitution.

Sally Blackmun, an abortion-rights activist and daughter of Justice Harry Blackmun, who authored the *Roe v. Wade* opinion, recounts how personal considerations entered into her father's thinking on the matter. She recalls that he often discussed the broad issues involved in his cases with his family "around the dinner table," and says that "he really struggled with *Roe v. Wade.*" At one point, when the family was in the middle of a meal together, Justice Blackmun asked Sally and her two sisters how they thought the case should be decided. They said that they favored the plaintiff. Appearing to take partial credit for the historic Supreme Court decision, Sally suggests that her father was certainly influenced by "his three daughters and an outspoken, independent wife."[2] And although Justice Blackmun's written decision cites a right of privacy that he found in the Fourteenth Amendment to the Constitution, his daughter maintains that he also viewed *Roe* as "an opportunity to give women rights that will emancipate them." Noting that her father had spent nine years working as general counsel for the Mayo Clinic, Sally Blackmun concludes that this period of his life "gave him the opportunity to see firsthand the aftereffects of botched illegal abortions."[3]

While we cannot know for certain what Justice Blackmun saw from his office at Mayo, we can infer from his own writings and comments about *Roe* that he was exactly as his daughter said: a staunch defender of a woman's right to choose. And while we also cannot be sure that Justice Blackmun's motivation was to "emancipate women" by striking down state abortion laws, we do know that legal scholars have made similar statements about the 1973 decision. The constitutional-law expert Bernard Siegan, for instance, believes that some of the justices, rather than engaging in a careful reading of the Constitution to guide them, made a political decision based upon their own personal beliefs. In his book *The Supreme Court's Constitution,* Professor Siegan suggests that in the case of *Roe v. Wade,* "a major problem confronted by the majority Justices was how best to rationalize constitutionally this enormously important decision, destined to strike down, in whole or in part, the statutes of every state in the Union." Siegan concludes that instead of interpreting a particular provision of the Constitution as requiring invalidation of a statute, the justices sought to find a constitutional basis for a decision they had already determined in advance. In his dissent, in fact, Justice Byron White criticized the decision as "an exercise in raw judicial power."[4]

Regardless of the motivations of the justices, it is important to continue examining the politics that shaped the abortion laws of the past so that we can better understand how such laws are being shaped today. While it is easy for the pro-life side to blame the Supreme Court for ushering in the era of abortion on demand through *Roe v. Wade,* the reality is that a decade of intense politics surrounding abortion helped make that ruling inevitable. As early as 1964, opinion leaders in states like New York and California had already begun to reform their states' abortion laws. By 1973, nineteen states had modified their abortion laws to allow for increased access to abortion, and there was every expectation that additional states would soon follow, reflecting the changing attitudes and emerging political power of the feminist movement.[5] Without the Supreme Court's intervention, access to abortion might well have expanded to additional states because of the momentum that abortion politics had gained; but we will never know because *Roe v. Wade* ended the debate.

The following chapters will look closely at the forces behind the politics of abortion in our recent past and in the present. *Roe v. Wade* was important for many reasons, but primarily because, as one participant in the debate has noted, the Supreme Court effectively "radicalized the abortion debate by denying to the pro-life side the ordinary tools of politics." The declaration that abortion was for all practical purposes an inalienable constitutional right "left the pro-life side unable to work the political trenches at the state level, or to push for statutory restrictions at the congressional level."[6] Yet the pro-life side has never really accepted the decision, while the pro-choice side believes they just need to "get over" their loss (as Justice Sandra Day O'Connor once suggested) and contemptuously dismisses their demands for equal protection under the law for the unborn.

Thus we remain deadlocked in a divisive culture war, though few on the pro-choice side will acknowledge this cultural divide. Instead, they locate the divisions elsewhere. During the 2004 Democratic presidential primary season, for instance, Senator John Edwards developed a compelling "two Americas" speech in which he claimed that we were hopelessly divided by class, with the rich leading lives of comfort and the poor struggling to survive. While Election Day revealed that Edwards—by then the losing vice presidential candidate—was correct about the existence of "two Americas," he was wrong about the main cause of division. His focus on a class divide that separated the rich from the poor missed the far deeper moral divide that cuts across class, racial, ethnic, political, and sexual lines. In fact, the Kerry-Edwards campaign failed to recognize that the deepest divisions in America are over cultural and moral issues. This failure cost the Democrats the election.

It is not primarily race, gender, class, or geography that divides America; rather, it is a cultural discord that cuts across all these variables. Many traditional, churchgoing middle- or upper-class people now find that they have much more in common with working-class churchgoing people than they do with their economically similar neighbors who do not attend church. Many professionals now find that although they may share an occupation and a social class with their fellow lawyers or physicians, they seek out social relationships instead with those who share their beliefs, attitudes, and values on a number of cultural subjects—including abortion. They nourish these friendships because they see their identity in terms of moral and cultural values, not social class or occupation.[7]

Not since slavery and the rise of the abolitionist movement has there been so bitter a culture war in this nation. Each side lives in a separate world, barely understanding the concerns, beliefs, and behavior of the other. And there is no area where this is more apparent than in the issue of abortion. While one America thinks that the lives of the unborn must be protected, another America thinks that all women should have access to abortion on demand, no matter how late in the pregnancy. While one America believes that a decision for abortion should never be made by a child without parental involvement, another America believes that minor children should be allowed to make their own decisions about an abortion without parental interference. While one America believes it is wrong to distribute condoms to middle-school children, another America dismisses abstinence programs as hopelessly naïve and wants not only "comprehensive sex education" in the schools but also access to birth control and abortion for minor children through school-based programs. While one side is appalled by third-term abortion, the other side insists that even partial-birth abortion falls within a woman's right to choose.

Denied the ordinary tools of politics by *Roe v. Wade,* the pro-life side has had little recourse but to wage this culture war—the continuation of politics by other means (to borrow a phrase from Clausewitz). As a result, for more than thirty years the pro-life movement has used strategies of education, advocacy, and protest (mostly peaceful) to make its point. But over the past decade, these strategies have become ever more constricted by court-imposed limits on free speech and the right to assembly.[8] In the 1990s, what began as a nonviolent war of conscience for the pro-life community was pushed into violence by a few radical extremists on the margins of the movement. Perhaps the conflict should have been expected: as the sociologist James Davison Hunter reminds us, "culture wars always precede shooting wars." Hunter also notes that "the last time this country debated the issues of human life, personhood, liberty, and the rights of citizenship all together, the result was the bloodiest war ever to take place on this continent, the Civil War."[9]

The rhetoric around the abortion issue became especially inflammatory during the 2004 presidential elections and through the contentious debate surrounding the apparent qualms about abortion shared by President Bush's Supreme Court nominees, John Roberts and Samuel Alito. With the election and the Senate hearings into these nominees' views on this issue behind us, it seems like a good time to stop and ask, who is winning the abortion war?

In all wars, the losses, imagined or real, are used to mobilize those engaged in the fighting. In an attempt to rally the troops, those on both sides of the abortion debate often assume the mantle of victimhood. Noting that new state initiatives threaten to limit access to abortion, Gloria Feldt, the president of Planned Parenthood, describes a feminist community under siege in *The War on Choice.* Likewise, journalist William Saletan's *Bearing Right: How Conservatives Won the Abortion War* makes the counterintuitive claim that the pro-choice side has actually "lost" the battle for abortion rights to a cabal of conservatives. In response, those on the pro-life side point out how thoroughly the elite media have blocked out their views, and they note the casualty count of the unborn and the less visible toll in the damaged lives of the mothers, the fathers, and the people involved in the abortion industry as proof of the high cost of choice.

We should be able to turn to the social scientists to help us assess the progress in the culture wars surrounding abortion. But unfortunately, with a few exceptions, they have themselves enlisted in the pro-choice army, writing amicus briefs supporting a woman's right to choose or voting for resolutions supporting abortion in professional societies such as the American Sociological Association and the American Psychological Association. Even a group of historians have spoken out in favor of a woman's right to choose abortion, drafting and signing an amicus brief in *Webster v. Reproductive Health Services,* a 1989 Supreme Court challenge to *Roe v. Wade,* which strongly denounced any attempt to restrict a woman's right to abortion. Claiming to represent the informed historical position, these scholars argued that our country has "always" supported abortion in the past.[10]

Many sociologists, still mired in an antiquated Marxism, continue to regard race, class, and gender as the primary explanations for the ongoing social battles, and look dismissively upon the intellectual and organizational abilities of their pro-life adversaries. In *The Politics of Motherhood* (1985), for instance, the sociologist Kristin Luker, claiming to be a partisan of neutrality, refused to call the form of life that exists between conception and birth either an unborn child or pre-born life or even a fetus. Instead, she used the term "embryonic," explaining that "in political movements, language becomes politicized, so a choice of words is a choice of sides.... As a result, in referring to the form of life that exists between conception and birth, I will use the term embryo."[11] Preferring to be scientifically wrong rather than violate the tenets of feminist political correctness, Luker devoted her entire book to describing the politics that surround the nine-month gestation period of an "embryo." Even odder than her nomenclature is the fact that *The Politics of Motherhood* was widely praised, winning a major book award from the American Sociological Association.

Yet despite the strong pro-choice views of the academy as well as the media and other centers of elite opinion, the politics of abortion, so long tilted toward the pro-choice movement, have started to shift. The following chapters will frame this often slow-motion political change by looking at the influence of the advocates on both sides of the abortion wars, identifying their funding sources, their beneficiaries, and their political activities, in an attempt to measure their success in promoting new entitlements, new programs, and new policies. The central question to be answered is: Exactly who has gained the power to define and redefine the issues? Who is winning in the public-opinion and public-policy debates surrounding abortion? This book is a report from the trenches.

CHAPTER ONE

Looking for the Life of the Party

REVIEWING THE HISTORY of the Democratic Party, it is difficult to say exactly when it went from being the Party of the New Deal, Medicare, and Aid to Families with Dependent Children, to the Party of Abortion on Demand. Some might point to the 1992 Democratic National Convention, when a once-popular liberal leader within the party, Governor Robert Casey of Pennsylvania, was not only denied a speaking role but banished to the far corners of the cavernous convention hall because of his pro-life views. Others might point to the 2000 convention, when the one-time pro-life Catholic Kennedy family, represented by Caroline Kennedy Schlossberg and Senator Ted Kennedy, addressed the convention to reassure all those gathered that the Democratic Party would continue to provide women with the right to choose abortion—even into the ninth month, when the unborn child looks and acts exactly like a human being and can live and breathe if born. At that convention the party's nominee, Al Gore, formerly a pro-life advocate, shouted out his opposition to parental notification in the case of abortion for minors and embraced partial-birth abortion. By then, nearly every delegate in the convention hall was on the pro-choice side—and those that weren't simply kept quiet about it.

To understand precisely when the Democratic Party embraced

abortion as its reason for being, we would have to look even further back—to the 1960s, the earliest days of the pro-choice movement, when a few activists teamed up with feminists and liberal church leaders, including pro-choice priests, to adopt an agenda that would ultimately force the Democratic Party to undergo the political equivalent of a sex-change operation.

In a long-forgotten meeting at the Kennedy compound in Hyannisport, on a hot summer day in 1964, the Kennedy family and their advisers and allies were coached by leading theologians and Catholic college professors to accept and promote abortion with a "clear conscience." Albert Jonsen a former Jesuit, recalls how this happened:

> In July, 1964, Jesuit priest, Fr. Joseph Fuchs, renowned Catholic moral theologian and a professor at the Gregorian University in Rome, was among the guest faculty of an ethics course I was teaching at the summer session at the University of San Francisco. Walking across campus one morning, Fr. Fuchs hailed me and told me that he had, on the previous day, received a phone call inviting him to join several other leading theologians in a meeting with Senator Ted Kennedy and Robert Kennedy at Hyannisport. Robert Kennedy was running for the New York Senate seat, and the Kennedy family and their political advisors wished to discuss the position that a Catholic politician should take on abortion.... Two days later, the distinguished German theologian and I, the American novice, traveled to Cape Cod to join Catholic theologians, Fr. Robert Drinan, then dean of Boston College Law School; Fr. Richard McCormick, Fr. Charles Curran; and a bishop whose name I do not recall. Our colloquium at Hyannisport, as I recall it, was influenced by Jesuit, Fr. John Courtney Murray's position and reached the conclusion that Catholic politicians in a democratic polity might advocate legal restriction on abortion, but in so doing might tolerate legislation that would permit abortion under certain circumstances if political efforts to repress this moral error led to greater perils to social peace and order. This position, which of course, is much more nuanced than I have stated, seems to have informed the politics of the Kennedys.[1]

Another Jesuit who helped redefine abortion for the Kennedy family at that meeting in Hyannisport was Fr. Giles Milhaven, who later recalled at a 1984 breakfast briefing of Catholics for a Free Choice:

> Having been asked to make a presentation this morning on Catholic options in public policy on abortion I cannot but recall the last time I was invited to do so.... I remember it vividly. Other theologians and I were driving down Route 3 to Cape Cod with Bob Drinan at the wheel. We were to meet with the Senators Kennedy and the Shrivers at their request. I remember it vividly because the traffic lanes were jammed and halted, presumably because of an accident ahead and Bob Drinan drove 60 miles an hour down the breakdown lane. Despite my misgivings each time we swept around a curve, we theologians arrived safely at the Kennedy compound..... The theologians worked for a day and a half among ourselves at a nearby hotel. In the evening we answered questions from the Kennedys and the Shrivers. Though the theologians disagreed on many a point, they concurred on certain basics...and that was that a Catholic politician could in good conscience vote in favor of abortion.

This Catholic cover for the right to abortion was soon enhanced by the pro-choice voting behavior of a Jesuit member of Congress, Fr. Robert Drinan, who served as an elected Democratic representative from 1970 until 1980. Throughout his tenure in Congress, Fr. Drinan could be counted on to provide some of the most extreme pro-choice votes. By the early 1970s, opposition to abortion among the Catholic laity—long a key constituency for the Democrats—was effectively neutralized and Catholic leaders helped build the foundation for the party's reincarnation as the party of abortion. The editor of *Catholic World News* sadly pointed out the irony of Democrats and Catholics collaborating in this way: "Long planned, hard won, fiercely defended, abortion-on-demand is the Catholic gift to American public life, perhaps our Church's only enduring political achievement."[2]

What was clear then and is even clearer today as we look back on those days is that the Kennedys were looking for a way to meet the growing interest in legalized abortion while still maintaining their appeal to their Catholic base. In meeting the nascent "demand" for legalized abortion by a small number of influential feminists and abortion-industry advocates, Robert Kennedy and his brother Ted faced a much more complex cultural issue than their brother, President John F. Kennedy, ever did. In fact, there is no public record of any statement by President Kennedy on the subject of abortion; it simply was not an issue throughout his political career. Before his assassination in 1963, no major political, social, or religious groups advocated legal abortion. Even the fledgling women's movement, including its founding document, Betty Friedan's *Feminine Mystique,* avoided the subject.

All that began to change as a few radical feminists joined with a few aspiring abortion-industry capitalists to begin defining abortion as a right—an event as significant as the Kennedys signing on. The affluent abortion proponent and entrepreneur Larry Lader partnered with his friend and Greenwich Village neighbor Dr. Bernard Nathanson, a gynecologist and abortion provider, to become the true leaders of this new movement. For Lader, the abortion issue was one whose political significance went far deeper than any concerns about the income potential. Having worked with Vito Marcantonio, the only Communist ever to be elected to the U.S. House of Representatives, Lader was an ardent feminist and a great admirer of Margaret Sanger. Writing about those early days in his book *The Hand of God,* Nathanson describes Lader as being "obsessed" with abortion:

> Larry and I soon were spending a great deal of time in each other's company.... Our subject was invariably abortion, if not directly then indirectly. With the election of the allegedly conservative Richard Nixon in 1968, we counted ourselves set back temporarily, but certainly not discouraged or defeated. When Martin Luther King and Robert Kennedy were assassinated in the same year, we discussed these monumental events primarily as whether they were good or bad for the abortion revolution that we were by this time scheming. Even Detroit Tigers' Denny McLain's heroic thirty game winning season (a feat no major league pitcher had brought off in thirty five years) had to be analyzed through the abortion prism.[3]

Nathanson recalls being "dragooned into planning political strategy with Lader." By 1969 they were setting the agenda for a meeting of the leading national pro-abortion figures to take place in Chicago. Out of that meeting would emerge what is today one of the biggest contributors to the Democratic Party, the National Association for Repeal of Abortion Laws (NARAL), later changed to the National Abortion Rights Action League, which today calls itself NARAL Pro-Choice America. Nathanson says that in order to accomplish the goal of abortion on demand, they "put out feelers to Betty Friedan and her corps of feminists to join us in the revolution...and crushing the dinosaurs in the movement.... Lader, I and a handful of others such as Howard Moody, then pastor of the Judson Memorial Church in Manhattan's Greenwich Village, were the radicals, the Bolsheviks. We would settle for nothing less than striking down all existing abortion statutes and substituting abortion on demand."[4]

The next step was approaching the media and designing a clever public-relations campaign. Nathanson writes that in the sixties, "the media trenches were peopled with young, cynical, politically case hardened, well educated radicals who were only too anxious to upset the status quo, roil the waters and rattle the cages of authority. Something mysterious but momentous had happened with the historical confluence of the assassination of John F. Kennedy, the torturous slow descent into the Vietnam quagmire, and the coming into political age of the baby boomer generation."[5]

With the Kennedys and other liberals in the Democratic Party watching, the first target of opportunity for Lader and Nathanson was the New York State statute prohibiting abortion. Nathanson recalls that Larry Lader knew that the governor of New York, Nelson Rockefeller, a liberal Republican, would not veto a bill striking down this law and he might very well apply discreet pressure to those legislators who seemed ambivalent. The media spotlight on a challenge to the abortion laws through a lawsuit (*Abramowicz v. Lefkowitz,* 1970) inspired three hundred women along with Assemblywoman Constance Cook to force a bill to repeal the anti-abortion laws onto the floor of the New York State legislature. The bill provided for legal abortion on demand during the first twenty-four weeks of pregnancy. After five hours of debate in the state senate it was passed by a vote of 31 to 26; then it moved to the assembly, where the vote resulted in a tie: 74 to 74. That would have been a defeat for the bill, but George Michaels, an assemblyman from Auburn in upstate New York who had originally voted "No" on the bill, changed his vote. Tearfully claiming that his family had encouraged him to support the bill, George Michaels became an instant "hero" for the pro-choice side. But he also became a pariah in his own district. A Democrat from a largely conservative and Republican district, Michaels had been elected on the votes of his Catholic constituency, a group accounting for about 65 percent of the city of Auburn. Still a staunchly pro-life party, the Democratic Party in Auburn denied him what otherwise would have been a routine renomination three months after his momentous vote on legalized abortion. After his defeat in the primary, he never again held public office.

Still, Michaels is remembered today among the Democratic elite as one of the most courageous men of his time. In 2002, the John F. Kennedy Profile in Courage Award was posthumously given to Michaels for striking down abortion laws in New York. The prizewinning essay by a high school student on the assemblyman's courageous actions was read at the Profile in Courage Award ceremony at the John F. Kennedy Library Foundation. Emily Ullman's essay lauded the pro-choice pioneer as having "performed an act of political courage in which his loyalty to his nation triumphed over all personal and political considerations."[6]

The Kennedys, like the party they dominated for so long, had come full circle. At the 1964 meeting with Catholic theologians at Hyannisport, Ted and Robert Kennedy had been interested in the connection between abortion and their liberal constituency within the party; yet they remained reluctant to commit themselves. More than five years later, in 1971, a full year after New York had legalized abortion, Senator Ted Kennedy was still championing the rights of the unborn. In a letter to a constituent dated August 3, 1971, he wrote:

> While the deep concern of a woman bearing an unwanted child merits consideration and sympathy, it is my personal feeling that the legalization of abortion on demand is not in accordance with the value which our civilization places on human life. Wanted or unwanted, I believe that human life, even at its earliest stages, has certain rights which must be recognized—the right to be born, the right to love, the right to grow old. On the question of the individual's freedom of choice there are easily available birth control methods and information which women may employ to prevent or postpone pregnancy. But once life has begun, no matter what stage of growth, it is my belief that termination should not be decided merely by desire.... When history looks back to this era it should recognize this generation as one which cared about human beings enough to halt the practice of war, to provide decent living for every family, and to fulfill its responsibility to its children from the very moment of conception.[7]

Kennedy was not the only Democrat to be wary of the issue in the 1970s. While some members of the party claimed that it was their democratic duty to represent their constituents' views, whatever their own private qualms, in fact mainstream Democrats in the 1970s were overwhelmingly anti-abortion. Even into the 1980s, most Democratic leaders remained publicly ambivalent about it. Indeed, in the decade following *Roe v. Wade,* pro-life Democrats formed a substantial portion of the party's membership in the United States Congress and Senate. Responding to the attitudes of their constituents, high-profile Democrats such as Jesse Jackson, Al Gore, and Bill Clinton were strongly pro-life. (Jackson once observed that the "privacy" argument used to justify the *Roe* decision was "the premise of slavery." Relating the right to abortion to the right to keep slaves, Jackson noted that "one could not protest the existence or treatment of slaves on the plantation because that was private and therefore outside of your right to be concerned.")[8]

But in the 1980s, the influence of the pro-life Democrats in the party declined considerably as the pro-choicers' fundraising abilities increased exponentially. Clinton, Jackson, Gore, and others abandoned their pro-life position in favor of the more pragmatic and increasingly more lucrative pro-choice position. But while it is rare to hear a pro-life voice from the Democratic Party today, it was actually not so long ago that many within the party still expressed concern about the pro-choice direction that their political leaders were taking. Throughout the 1980s, a series of articles highlighted the deep divisions that were emerging in the decade following *Roe v. Wade.* In September 1980, for instance, *The Progressive* published an article by Mary Meehan entitled "Abortion: The Left Has Betrayed the Sanctity of Life," expressing dismay that the left was ignoring the plight of the unborn: "The traditional mark of the Left had been its protection of the underdog, the weak, and the poor. The unborn child is the most helpless form of humanity, even more in need of protection than the poor tenant farmer or the mental patient or the boat people on the high seas. It is out of character for the Left to neglect the weak and the helpless."[9]

In October 1980, Pax Christi USA, a Catholic peace organization that includes feminists and socialists, approved what they called an "anti-abortion revolution" by a virtually unanimous vote at their national assembly. That same year, the "progressive" Christian magazine *Sojourners* featured Daniel Berrigan, Shelley Douglass, and Jesse Jackson, among others, arguing against abortion.[10]

Jay Sykes, who led Eugene McCarthy's 1968 antiwar campaign in Wisconsin and served as president of the American Civil Liberties Union of Wisconsin from 1968 to 1970, denounced liberals' support for abortion in a 1974 essay called "Farewell to Liberalism." Sykes lamented, "It is on the abortion issue that the moral bankruptcy of contemporary liberalism is most clearly exposed." He warned that "liberals' arguments in support of abortion could, without much refinement, be used to justify the legalization of infanticide."[11] Sykes was not alone in the early days of the ACLU's movement toward pro-choice advocacy. According to Mary Meehan, who had done extensive research on the ACLU position on abortion, Sykes was one of many ACLU members and supporters who felt uncomfortable about abortion, regarding it as killing. Reviewing the organization's own archives at Princeton University, Meehan found that the ACLU's abortion policy was shaped by dedicated lobbying on the part of a few of its leading members, who carefully chose the terms of the debate: "By using emotional appeals, selecting and often distorting statistics, and evading discussion of evidence about the humanity of the unborn, they enlisted their powerful group onto the side of abortion. Yet there has been internal dissent from ACLU abortion policy from the beginning."[12]

A few dissident voices on the left stubbornly continued to argue the pro-life position throughout the 1980s. Rosemary Bottcher, a columnist for the *Tallahassee Democrat* in the 1980s, drew a parallel between abortion and discrimination against women: "Pro-abortion feminists resent the discrimination against a whole class of humans because they happen to be female, yet they themselves discriminate against a whole class of humans because they happen to be very young. They resent the fact that the value of a woman is determined by whether some man wants her, yet they declare that the value of an unborn child is determined by whether some woman wants him. They resent that women have been 'owned' by their husbands, yet insist that the unborn are 'owned' by their mothers."[13] Bottcher decried the inconsistencies in the liberal position: "The same people who organized a boycott of the Nestle

Company for its marketing of infant formula in underdeveloped lands would have approved of the killing of those exploited infants only a few months before. The same people who talk incessantly of human rights are willing to deny the most helpless and vulnerable of all human beings the most important right of all."[14]

Writing in *Religious Socialism* in 1981, Julie Loesch, the founder of Pro-Lifers for Survival, took notice of how "progressive" opponents of abortion had entered into a bipartisan alliance: "Soon after the 1973 *Roe v. Wade* decision, one of the most progressive Senate Democrats, Harold Hughes, joined one of the most progressive Republicans, Mark Hatfield, in co-sponsoring a Human Life Amendment. Both were opponents of the Vietnam War. Both opposed abortion because of, not despite their other political views."[15]

This Republican-Democrat pro-life coalition of the early 1980s could exist because abortion had not yet become the defining commitment of the Democratic Party. By 1984, however, Democratic delegates to the national convention in San Francisco were overwhelmingly pro-choice—even though mainstream Democratic voters then were not. The National Organization for Women had a strong presence, opening a generous purse for pro-choice candidates while "gut-checking" opponents on the abortion issue. Also present were Catholics for a Free Choice, a group funded by the Ford Foundation in 1973 to make the case that the Catholic hierarchy did not speak for Catholics on abortion; it was spun off from the National Organization for Women under the leadership of Joan Harriman, Patricia Fogarty McQuillan, and Meta Mulcahay.

Catholics for a Free Choice has always staged dramatic public events, often in reaction to some decision made by a bishop. (The most famous of these occurred in 1974 when Patricia Fogarty McQuillan crowned herself pope on the steps of St. Patrick's Cathedral in New York on the first anniversary of the *Roe* decision.)[16] But it was not until 1982, when Catholics for a Free Choice hired a new and much stronger president, Frances Kissling, that the organization became a force within the Democratic Party. Having seen the success of NOW in penetrating the party's top echelon, Kissling knew that power flowed from money and made it her mission to funnel as much money as possible to Democratic pro-choice politicians while giving the dwindling numbers of pro-life Democrats nothing. Kissling also spent large amounts of money on various media campaigns to promote her cause—and herself. In one of her most dramatic and successful actions, Kissling purchased a full-page advertisement in the *New York Times* in 1984, asserting that "A Diversity of Opinions Regarding Abortion Exists among Committed Catholics." Signers of the ad included Catholic dissident theologians, priests, nuns, academics, and other high-profile dissenters within the Church.

While the Vatican responded strongly by denouncing the ad and a bishop excommunicated one of its supporters, the San Diego politician Lucy Killea, the controversy generated enormous media attention for years. Killea is still remembered fondly within the pro-choice community today. The *San Diego Union-Tribune* recently provided a "retrospective review" lauding Killea's courage and providing readers with an update on her current work. Throughout the country, the response from the Catholic hierarchy to the *New York Times* ad emboldened the radical pro-choice community and mobilized even those in the middle on the abortion issue.[17]

The delegates to the 1984 Democratic National Convention were in synch with pro-choice groups like NOW and Catholics for a Free Choice. In fact, when a poll was conducted at the convention asking whether there should be a constitutional amendment outlawing abortion, only 9 percent of all the delegates supported such an amendment, even though it was supported by 46 percent of all Democrats nationwide. Likewise, while the Black Caucus in 1984 advocated a "right" to abortion, 62 percent of blacks opposed abortion.[18] It was clear that the pro-choice elites had hijacked the Democratic Party.

In September 26, 1986, Governor Bill Clinton was sailing against the wind when he assured the head of the Arkansas chapter of the National Right to Life Committee, "I am opposed to abortion and to government funding of abortion."[19] Even today, Clinton seems occasionally conflicted about when life actually begins. In his book *My Life*, he writes, "Everyone knows life begins biologically at conception. But, no one knows when biology turns into humanity."[20] Still, such concerns did not keep him from vetoing a ban on partial-birth abortion—when an unborn child's body is partially delivered and then the child is killed outside the mother's body—during his presidency, saying that he wanted to "keep government out of private, personal matters.... I believe that the ultimate choice should remain a matter for a woman to decide in consultation with her conscience, her doctor, and her God."

By the 1992 Democratic National Convention, pro-choice voices within the party had effectively been silenced. The Democratic governor of Pennsylvania, Robert Casey, was not even allowed to address the delegates because of his pro-life stance. "Casey's party treated him with disdain," remarked Nat Hentoff in the *New Republic.*

> As the 1992 Democratic Convention in New York approached, Casey told me he had expected, in light of his policy accomplishments and political loyalty, to be a speaker, maybe even the keynote speaker. But, not only was he not appointed to be the keynote speaker, Casey was not even allowed to speak at the Convention. In fact, he and his Pennsylvania delegation were exiled to the farthest reaches of Madison Square Garden. It did not matter that, under his leadership, state contracts to minority and women-owned firms in Pennsylvania had increased more than 1,500 percent in five years, or that he had appointed more female Cabinet members than any Democratic governor in the country, or that he had appointed the first black woman ever to sit on a state Supreme Court. Ron Brown, chief convention organizer and the Democratic Party's symbol of minority inclusion, told Casey, "Your views are out of line with those of most Americans."[21]

Casey had the misfortune of being present during the great shift in the Democratic Party, as Hentoff explained:

> In the early '90s, the Democrats, seeking the votes of upper-middle-class Republican women, were de-emphasizing economic protection and stressing cultural libertarianism. And, just to make sure everyone got the message, Democratic strategists invited Kathy Taylor, a pro-choice Pennsylvania Republican who helped defeat Casey's progressive tax reforms, to the New York convention. She appeared onstage pledging the National Abortion Rights Action League's allegiance to the Clinton-Gore team. The DNC officials sent Taylor, with a camera crew in tow, to find Casey in "Outer Mongolia," as Casey later described his inauspicious place at the Conventional Hall, to further humiliate him.[22]

Robert Casey never left the Democratic Party, although it certainly appeared that the party had left him. Like some Trotskyite sects of the past, isolated pockets of the left continued to support him in his lonely stance. In the fall of 1992, for instance, Nat Hentoff helped organize a lecture in New York on the topic "Can a Liberal Be Pro-Life?" and invited Casey to speak. In *U.S. News & World Report,* the columnist John Leo described the chaos that ensued: "About a hundred shrieking protestors stopped the speech. According to the *Voice* report, half were from ACT UP (the AIDS advocacy group) and radical feminist groups, and half were assorted radicals, some protesting the pending execution in Pennsylvania of Mumia Abu Jamal, former Black Panther convicted of killing a police officer. As Hentoff introduced Casey, the chant started: Racist, sexist, antigay, Governor Casey go away."[23] According to Leo, the screaming, chanting and whistling lasted thirty-five minutes, until Casey gave up and left the platform. Hentoff called it the ugliest crowd he had ever seen.

When Governor Casey died in 2000, the *New York Times,* the *Washington Post,* and hundreds of Associated Press news stories as well as major media networks including CNN all described him as "a conservative Democrat" despite the fact that Casey had championed many liberal initiatives, including making Pennsylvania one of the first states to mandate help for young, disabled children; setting up a model child-care program for state workers; and creating a program to provide health care to every uninsured child in Pennsylvania up to the age of six. Casey had been lauded by the National Women's Caucus for his willingness to appoint women to cabinet positions and for increasing the participation of women and minorities in state construction contracts from 1 percent to 15 percent. A liberal in his political life, in death Casey became a "conservative"—tantamount to a malediction—because, as the media described it, "he relentlessly berated his party and its 1992 presidential candidate, Bill Clinton, for abandoning its traditional constituencies with what Casey called an abortion on demand philosophy."[24] The Associated Press obituary quoted Casey as lamenting, "My party, the Democratic Party, should be the protector and claims to be the protector of the powerless. It is time to get back to what this country is all about, protecting all of the powerless.... And that includes unborn children."[25]

By the 2000 elections, the Democratic Party had become almost obsessively focused on "choice." Still, the Democratic presidential candidate had a problem. As a Democratic congressman for a conservative Tennessee district in the early 1980s, Al Gore had amassed an 84 percent right-to-life voting record. Later, as he won a Senate seat and became a national figure, he changed his position, and while running for president he claimed that he would do everything in his power to prevent *Roe v. Wade* from being overturned. Still, it was not easy for Gore—there was a long pro-life paper trail that followed his nomination. And, although few media outlets reminded potential voters of Gore's pro-life stand, he was occasionally forced to respond to critics of his reversal. The *Boston Globe* recalled Gore's prior pro-life record by publishing a letter that Gore had written to a constituent in 1984 when he was representing Tennessee in the House of Representatives: "It is my deep personal conviction that abortion is wrong. Let me assure you that I share your belief that innocent human life must be protected, and I have an open mind about how to further this goal." In a second letter to a constituent in 1987, he again wrote that abortion is "the taking of a human life."[26] When asked about these views on the *David Frost Show* in 1992, Gore responded that he no longer used such phrases in letters because they are so "loaded with political charge."[27] He added:

> I think many of us have mixed feelings, because there are two questions involved. The first question is how you feel about an abortion in a given set of circumstances. And the second question is who makes the decision? And regardless of how you and I might feel about the rightness or wrongness of a given decision in a particular set of circumstances, I believe that the government ought not to have the right to order a woman to accept its judgment about how to weigh the different aspects of the decision, and order the woman to make the decision that government says she has to make, instead of leaving the decision to her. I have always believed that.[28]

Although Gore had to acknowledge during the 2000 campaign that at one time he had opposed public funding for abortion, he claimed that this stand did not mean he had not supported abortion. At the Democrat debate in Los Angeles on March 1, 2000, he promised: "I will defend a woman's right to choose, regardless of her economic circumstances. I will not allow *Roe v. Wade* to be overturned. Early in my career, I opposed public funding for abortion. But, I never supported the criminalization of abortion. In those days, many of us saw the phrase pro-choice as referring to supporting *Roe v. Wade*." Gore continued to claim—despite all evidence to the contrary—that he had always been "pro-choice."[29]

While all of the Democratic candidates in 2004 were pro-choice, abortion had become such a litmus test that some candidates scrambled to show that they were *more* pro-choice than the others. In this wholesale revisionism, *à la* Gore, on the subject of earlier qualms about abortion, the long-shot candidate Dennis Kucinich had trouble competing. As a congressman he had voted in favor of a ban on partial-birth abortion, and in favor of a ban on funding for family planning in foreign aid. Kucinich also voted to bar the transport of minors to obtain an abortion in another state, and to make it a federal crime to harm the fetus while committing other crimes. In fact, during his first three terms in Congress, Kucinich had compiled so consistent a pro-life voting record that he earned a 95 percent rating from the National Right to Life Committee in 2000.[30] Yet beginning in 2002, perhaps in anticipation of his run for the presidency, Kucinich began the journey from pro-life to pro-choice, so that by the time of the 2004 elections, NARAL Pro-Choice America gave Kucinich a 100 percent pro-choice voting record. For the pro-choice community, Kucinich's finest moment came when he voted against banning partial-birth abortion.[31]

Kate Michelman, president of NARAL Pro-Choice America, gave political cover to Kucinich: "The transformations of Kucinich and past pro-life Democrats are the opposite of being political. When they were being anti-choice, it was the political thing to do maybe. At that time, their position was expected of them to be anti-choice. I think they have thought a lot more about this issue and came to the decision after a great deal of thought and not as a reflex."[32]

Richard Gephardt, who had been widely considered the frontrunner in Iowa because of his 1988 victory there and his longtime union support, also had problems trying to explain away some of his own pro-life votes. In fact, NARAL Pro-Choice America was so concerned about Gephardt's willingness to vote seven times in favor of banning partial-birth abortion that it gave him a pro-choice voting record of only 30 percent. In 2002, Gephardt had voted against funding for health-care providers who do not offer abortion information, and he voted against a ban on funding of family planning in U.S. aid abroad. He also voted against making it a federal crime to harm a fetus while committing other crimes and against barring the transport of minors to another state to obtain an abortion. Yet for NARAL Pro-Choice America, any vote against an unlimited right to abortion qualified a politician for a pro-life label. In the past, an organization like NARAL would have been a fringe group; but changes in the Democratic Party over the years have placed it at the heart of the party. For a Democrat like Gephardt, a low pro-choice rating from NARAL could end any hope for the party's nomination in the primary.

Candidate Wesley Clark certainly bore that reality in mind as he became perhaps the most radically pro-choice candidate in the history of presidential politics. Throughout the primary season, Clark tried constantly to distance himself from his Catholic upbringing and often stated that abortion is a matter of human rights, not of Catholic doctrine. At one point during the primaries, Clark celebrated the thirty-first anniversary of *Roe v. Wade* by appearing at a breakfast fundraiser sponsored by the Planned Parenthood of Northern New England Action Fund. At the breakfast, Clark declared that "no one has the right to come between a woman, her doctor, her family, and her God. Choice is a fundamental Constitutional right, plain and simple. And my commitment to choice doesn't stop with reproductive choice. I am going to fight to expand choice for women and men in all aspects of their lives—in the home, the workplace, and everywhere else." Attempting to bolster his argument, he asserted: "I stood up for human rights in Bosnia. I stood up for human rights in Kosovo. And I'll stand up for human rights here in America."[33]

During an interview with the editorial board of the *Manchester Union,* Clark pledged that he would not appoint any judge who was not "100 percent pro-choice." He then went on to say that *Roe v. Wade* entitles a woman to abort a child up to the moment of birth—even if the mother is in labor when she makes the decision. This exchange took place between Clark and the *Manchester Union's* publisher, Joseph McQuaid:[34]

Clark: I don't think you should get the law involved in abortion.
McQuaid: At all?
Clark: Nope
McQuaid: Anything up to delivery?
Clark: Nope. Nope.
McQuaid: Anything up to the head coming out of the womb?
Clark: I say that it's up to the woman and her doctor, her con-
science....

Other candidates, even those with a position on the issue close
to Clark's, had learned, after decades of political experience, how to
condemn abortion while at the same time condoning it.[35] For
example, Al Sharpton said in his 2002 book, *Al on America,* "My
religion says that abortion is wrong. And, while I may believe that life
begins when the sperm meets the egg, and that only God should
decide whether to take a life, I will not stand in the way of a woman's
right to choose. If women do not have a right to choose, then it is a
civil rights violation." Sharpton also wrote, "I would only appoint
justices to the Supreme Court who are for women having the right
to choose whether or not they will have an abortion. Now, I can
believe something without having to impose my beliefs on others.
That's true separation of church and state."[36]

In contrast to the inexperienced Wesley Clark, Sharpton and
most of the Democratic primary candidates were successful in convincing voters that although they might view abortion as a "sadness,"
they were willing to support a woman's right to choose. No candidate walked this line better than John Kerry. Even though Kerry
constantly referred to his Catholic religion and his years as an altar
boy, he was, with the exception of Clark, the most consistently pro-
choice candidate from the Democratic Party. With a 100 percent
pro-choice vote rating from the pro-choice groups including
NARAL and Planned Parenthood, Kerry had always been counted
on to supply the needed pro-choice vote on all bills even remotely
related to abortion.

In fact, candidate Kerry tried to elevate abortion to the position of the most important question facing the country. In an
interview for the *Washington Post,* he promised to make abortion "a
defining issue in the debates" with President Bush.[37] When CNN's
Larry King asked him what his first executive order as president

would be, Kerry's response had nothing to do with matters like the war on terror, the economy, education, or health care. Instead, Kerry replied that for him the most important executive order he could issue would be to "Remove the Mexico City policy on the gag rule regarding funding for abortion counseling so that we can take a responsible position on family planning."[38]

As a freshman senator in 1984, Kerry declared abortion a basic human right and later asserted that abortion should be moved into "the mainstream of medical practice."[39] The journalist Peter Kirsanow also pointed out that Kerry's voting record matched his rhetoric: "He voted six times against bills that would have banned partial birth abortion, maintaining that there is no such thing as a partial birth. Kerry has voted three times against bills requiring parental consent or notification for a minor to get an abortion. Kerry also opposed making it a federal crime for anyone other than a parent to transport a minor across state lines to obtain an abortion in a state that allows abortion to minors without parental permission."[40] Not only did Kerry vote at least twenty-five times in favor of using taxpayer funds to pay for abortions in the United States, he vehemently opposed President Bush's restriction on federal funds to groups providing abortion counseling overseas. Kerry voted to kill an amendment that would prohibit the United Nations Population Fund from providing funds to organizations in China involved in coercive abortions and involuntary sterilization; and he also voted against an amendment to prohibit federal funds from being used to perform abortions or to provide abortion referrals at elementary and second schools.[41]

As the abortion candidate par excellence, Kerry may have been in perfect agreement with most of the delegates to the 2004 Democratic National Convention, but he was still out of step with most voters, however much the abortion debate may have shifted since that meeting at the Kennedy compound in 1964. The CBS News/*New York Times* delegate poll revealed that in 2004 almost twice as many Democratic delegates as Democratic voters thought that abortion should be permitted in all cases.[42] While Kerry opposed the Unborn Victims of Violence Act, also known as "Laci and Conner's Law" after Scott Petersen's victims, more than 80 percent of all voters support it. Likewise, while Kerry voted against all bans on partial-birth abortions, more than 70 percent of the public supports a ban on the grisly procedure.

Prior to the Democratic National Convention that year, the Democrats for Life of America held a convention dinner. Eunice Kennedy Shriver, sister of the late President John F. Kennedy and Senator Robert Kennedy, and probably the only pro-life Kennedy left in the family, attended the dinner. Ray Flynn, former mayor of Boston and ambassador to the Vatican, addressed the pro-life gathering and admonished his party that they were "out of step with the American people" when it came to pro-life values. And while the majority of the members of the Democratic Party may not support pro-life causes, a 2004 Zogby poll found that 43 percent of Democrats agree with the statement that abortion "destroys a human life and is manslaughter."

Democrats for Life, founded in 1999, tries to pull the Democratic Party back from the abortion precipice; but the party finds this pro-life organization embarrassing. In 2003, the chairman of the Democratic National Committee, Terry McAuliffe, refused to allow it to be linked on the DNC website. Mark Shields, a pro-life columnist, pointed out that the website included 261 links to groups as varied as the Forest Service and the Oneida Indian Organization and Easter Seals—yet Democrats for Life was considered beyond the pale.[43] Following the publication of the Shields piece, the DNC removed all 261 links.

Because of its marginalized status, Democrats for Life is grateful for any sign of affirmation at all within the party. And indeed, with the defeat of John Kerry, some Democratic leaders seemed for a short while to soften their stance on the pro-choice litmus test for candidates. Pro-choice stalwart Hillary Clinton began to describe abortion as a "sadness" in January 2005. The current Senate minority leader, Harry Reid of Nevada, a Mormon, has sometimes been described as "moderately pro-life." But this may be wishful thinking: Reid has continued to block parental notification laws and supports the Democratic commitment to abortion on demand.

In January 2005, pro-life Democratic voters were encouraged when a pro-life former Democratic representative, Tim Roemer, announced his candidacy to replace Terry McAuliffe as chairman of the Democratic National Committee. Pro-choice groups lashed out against Roemer, who ultimately was defeated by Howard Dean in the campaign for the chairmanship. Still, his candidacy was seen as a positive sign for pro-life Democrats. Eager for any positive signs, Democrats for Life applauds the smallest movement toward their side.*

But even a minimal debate within the party is resisted by NARAL's Kate Michelman, for whom the nomination of pro-life candidates "would mean that the party is abandoning its core values."[44] Michelman and others at the top of the party hierarchy seem not to understand that the way abortion became a "core value" for the Democrats—in the same sense that welfare assistance to the poor and medical assistance to the elderly once were—may be part of the story of the party's national decline.

The *New York Times* ran a piece early in 2005 warning that "For Democrats, Rethinking Abortion Runs Risks." The article pointed out that after the party was soundly defeated in the November 2004 elections, abortion received a sort of backhanded reconsideration. Senator Charles E. Schumer of New York, chairman of the Democratic Party's senatorial campaign committee, had actually encouraged Robert Casey Jr. to run in Pennsylvania as an opponent of abortion rights.[45] But as the *Times* noted, party loyalists were angered by such signs of pragmatism on the abortion issue.

Why? For one reason, because abortion-rights organizations are major donors to the Democratic Party. For example, Karen White, political director of Emily's List, a pro-abortion group that raises money for female candidates who support its positions, reacted to the possibility of a Casey candidacy by saying that her organization was "very excited" about backing his likely opponent, Barbara Hafer, a former Pennsylvania treasurer and a supporter of abortion rights. Emily's List, NARAL, Planned Parenthood, and other pro-abortion

---

*As the 2006 elections approach, the Democrats seem poised to nominate two pro-life candidates for the United States Senate, one in Pennsylvania and the other in Rhode Island. One of these candidates, Robert Casey Jr. (son of the pro-life former party leader, Governor Robert Casey) may run against the Republican Rick Santorum in the next Senate race in Pennsylvania. And in Rhode Island, a pro-abortion Republican, Senator Lincoln Chafee, may be unseated by a pro-life Democrat, Representative James Langevin. It is even possible that Republican pro-life voters will switch their party allegiance in order to vote for a pro-life candidate.

groups have responded aggressively to the tentative pro-life movement within the party. In fact, during the search for a national
Democratic chairman, Emily's List posted a rallying cry on its website: "We fought like mad to beat back the Republicans. Little did we
know that we would have just as much to fear from some within the
Democratic Party who seem to be using choice as a scapegoat for our
top of the ticket losses."[46] In an attempt to stop even the hint of
revisionism on abortion, Emily's List began to circulate a study it
commissioned by the pollster Mark Mellman indicating that abortion
"was not a factor in voters' decision-making in the November 2004
elections." And, in an effort to warn Democrats who might consider adopting a moderate position on the issue, Karen Pearl, interim
president of Planned Parenthood, threatened: "To the degree that
the Democrats move away from choice, that could be the real birth
of a third party movement."[47]

It is likely that the Democrats will indeed keep their commitment to the right to unlimited abortion on demand, if for no other
reason than the fact that the party cannot afford to lose the money
that the abortion groups raise for it. (*The New York Times* recently
reported that single-issue abortion-rights groups have given more
than twice as much to candidates for national office than groups
opposed to abortion.) In addition to Emily's List, which raised several million dollars for female candidates who support abortion
rights, donors like the George Soros, Ted Turner, Warren Buffet, and
David and Lucile Packard foundations bankroll pro-choice organizations, which in turn funnel more money to the Democratic Party.
Jane Fonda remains the biggest donor of all, having earmarked millions for the cause.[48]

Indeed, the National Abortion and Reproductive Rights
Action League has consistently provided tremendous support to pro-
choice candidates—mostly Democrats. In the 2000 election year,
NARAL reported nearly $6 million in independent expenditures in
support of pro-choice federal candidates. More than half of that was
donated to the presidential candidate Al Gore, who received $3.6
million. In addition, in 1999–2000, NARAL-PAC reported to the
Federal Elections Commission that it disbursed about $1.6 million
to candidates, party organizations, and other political action com-
mittees. It gave $463,261 to Democratic candidates and $29,699
to Republican candidates.[49]

NARAL has even done some creative accounting in order to move money to Democratic candidates. It received $3,075,000 from the group Pro-Choice Vote, whose only donor was Jane Fonda. (This "organization" seems to have been created simply as a way for Fonda to funnel money to NARAL.) Within thirty days of the organization's founding on September 12, 2000, Fonda contributed $12,235,000 to Pro-Choice Vote, which then transferred $3,075,000 to NARAL. In turn, NARAL reported making "independent expenditures" during that period in the amount of $5,289,836.[50] The $12 million from Fonda was in addition to the donations of $3,290,700 in 1999 and $1,799,466 in 2000 to NARAL from her then-husband's Turner Foundation for Proactive Reproductive Health Policy Programs.[51]

While it is clear that there has been a strong financial incentive for the Democratic Party to remain loyal to the abortion lobby, *Wall Street Journal* contributor Peggy Noonan believes that the party's obsession with abortion is more than a pragmatic desire to attract money, the mother's milk of politics. Noonan says that "abortion is the glue that holds the Democratic Party together. Without abortion to keep them together, the Democrats would fly apart into 50 small parties—Dems for free trade, Dems for protectionism; for quotas, for merit. All parties have divisions, the Republicans famously so, but Republicans have general philosophical views that keep them together and supported by groups that share their views. They're all united by, say, hostility to high taxes, but sometimes they have different reasons for opposing tax increases." In Noonan's analysis, the Democratic Party is "composed not of allied groups in pursuit of the same general principles but warring groups vying for money, power, a louder voice, and the elevation of their particular cause."[52] One thing they can all agree on is abortion.

But the Democratic Party's placation of and financial dependence on abortion-rights groups put it on a collision course with a political and demographic fact: a growing number of Americans are pro-life. While the majority of these are Republicans, a significant number of registered Democrats are becoming increasingly pro-life. In December 2004, the pollster John Zogby teamed up with Brad O'Leary of the O'Leary Report to examine the cultural differences in states that elected George Bush as president in 2000 and those that voted for Al Gore. The results were surprising to some: 68 percent of Republicans in the United States agreed with the statement that "abortion destroys a human life and is manslaughter," while 43 percent of Democrats also agreed. In addition, the Zogby poll showed that 22 percent of Americans indicated they were more interested in abortion restrictions than they had been five or ten years earlier.

Other polls show similar pro-life leanings for both Republicans and Democrats. An October 2003 ABC News/*Washington Post* poll, timed to coincide with the twenty-fifth anniversary of the papacy of John Paul II, found that a majority of Americans and Catholics believe abortion is morally unacceptable. Of all respondents, 58 percent said they thought abortion when the mother's life is not in danger was wrong; 66 percent of Catholics agreed. Only 39 percent of Americans and—contrary to what the Catholics for a Free Choice website proclaims—only 30 percent of Catholics regarded abortion as morally acceptable.[53] Statistics like these may make Democratic politicians question how they ever allowed pro-abortion groups to become the life of the party.

CHAPTER TWO

Race and the Politics of Abortion

A FEW YEARS AGO, several daily newspapers across the country published a syndicated cartoon consisting of three panels: one panel depicted a Ku Klux Klan rally, the second showed a Nazi rally, and the final one portrayed a pro-choice rally. At the top were the words: "Which of these kills more Blacks?"

Pro-choice feminists were furious about the cartoon and demanded an apology. In interviews following its publication, the cartoonist, Chuck Asay of the *Colorado Springs Gazette Telegraph,* said that the theme of this particular piece had emerged from his discussions with black clergy in the Colorado Springs area who had become concerned about the alarming abortion rates within the African American community. Asay's editors said they supported him because they believed that the cartoon breached no limit of decency or fairness. In fact, one of Asay's editors stated that he judged it to be an example of "African American advocacy."[1]

What Asay's editors didn't say, but no doubt knew, was that the statistics on race and abortion are indeed a concern for anyone who cares about the African American community. According to the Alan Guttmacher Institute, more than 43 percent of all African American pregnancies end in abortion. Since 1973, the number of abortions by African American women has totaled nearly twelve million. Every day in the United States, more than 1,500 African American women choose to end their pregnancies through abortion.[2] Although African Americans represent only 12 percent of the American population, they account for more than 35 percent of all abortions. As a result, the abortion rate (the number of abortions per 1,000 women ages 15 to 44 per year) for African American women is 2.9 times that of white women. Put another way, for every 1,000 African American women, 32 have abortions, as compared with 11 for every 1,000 white women. Comparing the number of abortions per 1,000 live births by race, we find that the abortion/birth ratio for white women is 184 abortions per 1,000 live births; for African American women, it is 543 abortions per 1,000 births. And African American women are also more likely to obtain the far riskier abortions late in their pregnancies, while white women desiring abortion are significantly more likely to obtain their abortions before sixteen weeks.

The continued inequality in access to health care may contribute to the high rate of late-term abortions among African American women. But the easy availability of abortion services within African American neighborhoods and the continued commitment by the pro-choice community to target African American women in their outreach also play a role in the racial disparity in abortion rates. And this disparity has increased steadily over the past few decades. In some localities, including Louisiana, Maryland, and Georgia, more than half of all abortions are now performed on African American women. In Mississippi, while African Americans represent 37 percent of the population, they account for 73 percent of the state's total number of abortions. African American women in New York City and in the state of New Jersey receive more than 47 percent of all abortions performed there.

Comparisons by race cannot be made in California because this state, unlike any other in the union, refuses to comply with requirements to report statistics on abortion. California's reporting requirement was enacted in 1967 as part of a larger abortion law called the Therapeutic Abortion Act. Yet even with the threat of losing federal funds, California has consistently refused to report its abortion data. Michael Quinn, the chief of California's Office of Health Information, was quoted in a Catholic newspaper account as saying, "California does not actively collect abortion statistics because they are highly sensitive and highly political."[3]

How right he is! Abortion data are sensitive because they reveal life-and-death decisions by women under a variety of pressures. It is likely that the pro-choice advocates in California do not want to publish the racial and ethnic demographics of abortion because the statistics would lend credence to what some in the African American and Latino communities throughout the country are calling racial and ethnic genocide.[4]

The Reverend Johnny Hunter of the organization Blacks for Life writes that "abortion is racism in its ugliest form. Because of some very suave planning by abortion supporters and providers, abortionists have eliminated more African American children than the KKK ever lynched.... Two hundred years ago our African American heritage was robbed by a group of elitist individuals who intentionally kept us ignorant concerning the devastating effects of slavery. Today, our heritage is being robbed by elitist individuals who have intentionally kept us ignorant concerning the devastating effect of abortion on our race."[5]

Like Hunter, the Reverend Clenard Childress Jr. of Montclair, New Jersey, president of the Northeast region of the Life Education and Research Network (LEARN), the nation's largest African American evangelical pro-life group, hopes to reduce the number of African American abortions by trying to "proclaim the message of life and to expose the vices of the abortion industry to the African American community." Childress believes that African American churches have been silent on the topic of abortion because of their close alliance with the Democratic Party: "Blacks embraced the Democrats' agenda because Democrats were viewed as facilitators of the civil-rights movement while Republicans were seen as those nasty white bigots who are out to oppress us."[6] But as a result, Childress points out, African Americans have also embraced an agenda that has contributed to the estimated 11,156,700 African American unborn children lost to abortion since 1973. (By comparison, AIDS has claimed 292,522 African American lives since 1973, violent crime 306,313, accidents 370,723, cancer 1,638,350, and heart disease 2,266,789 African American lives.)

Although Childress is a lifelong registered Democrat, he says that as a result of publicizing these figures in his church and elsewhere, he has been accused of "promoting a Republican platform." He maintains that his concern "for the life of my people" stems from his convictions as a pastor rather than politics. In an effort to educate African Americans about how abortion is affecting their community, Rev. Childress has developed a website, blackgenocide.org, that provides information about the continued commitment to a culture of death within the black community.[7] One of the facts he emphasizes is that more than 78 percent of Planned Parenthood's abortion centers are in or near minority communities.

The targeting of African Americans for abortion has a long history in the United States, beginning in the early 1900s with Margaret Sanger, the founder of Planned Parenthood. Sanger's involvement with eugenics, an attempt to control human reproduction in order to improve the quality of the race, led her to publish racist statements on the need to address the overbreeding of the "inferior races." From the beginning, birth control was especially appealing to eugenicists determined to check the climbing birthrates of the "unfit," including most importantly Negroes.

The Negro Project, a eugenics-movement initiative intended to promote population control through the sterilization of African Americans, was undertaken by Margaret Sanger in 1939 as a response to requests from some southern public-health officials. She believed that the "mass of Negroes" breeding in the South was a dysgenic horror, and therefore decided to work closely with religious leaders to help market her ideas about birth control as a "sacred choice." She devoted an entire chapter of her 1922 book, *The Pivot of Civilization,* to criticizing the dangers of the "overbreeding of the races." Because of this, Sanger championed the earliest family-planning clinics in African American neighborhoods like Harlem.

Sanger built upon the popularity of eugenics, which had become almost a religion among elites in the 1920s and early 1930s. In the earliest days of the fledgling birth-control movement, she focused her work and her rhetoric on trying to create a "superior race." Attracted, like Adolf Hitler, to Nietzsche's ideas about humanity as a work in progress and the need to create the godlike Superman, Sanger envisioned a new race of biologically superior creatures who would be as different from us as we are from apes. In her first book, *Woman and the New Race,* she advocated birth control and sterilization as tools to prevent the superior race from being "forced into a cradle race with rapidly breeding inferiors."[8] In 1939, she and the wealthy philanthropist Clarence Gamble produced a pamphlet called "Birth Control and the Negro," which asserted that the "poorer areas, particularly in the South, are producing alarmingly more than their share of future generations."[9]

The *Birth Control Review,* Sanger's magazine, often featured racists and eugenists, many of whom joined her in warning about the dangers of the "overbreeding" of the inferior races. For example, Lothrop Stoddard, a member of Sanger's board of directors, cautioned readers about "The Rising Tide of Color against White World-Supremacy," saying, "We must resolutely oppose both Asiatic permeation of white-race areas and Asiatic inundation of those non-white but equally non-Asiatic regions inhabited by the really inferior races." But Sanger was not content merely to publish racist propaganda; the magazine also made concrete policy proposals such as "the creation of what she called the moron communities, the forced production of children by the fit and the compulsory sterilization and even elimination of the 'unfit.'"[10]

Sanger was critical of the poor of all races. Indeed, in *The Pivot of Civilization* she argued that helping the poor by charity is socially harmful:

> My criticism of charity is not directed at the failure of philanthropy, but rather at its success. The dangers inherent in the very idea of humanitarianism and altruism, are dangers which have today produced their full harvest of human waste, of inequality and inefficiency…. Today, we may measure the evil effects of benevolence of this type, not merely upon those who have indulged in it, but upon the community at large. Organized charity is confronted with the problem of feeble mindedness and mental defect. But just as the State has so far neglected the problem of mental defect until this takes the form of criminal delinquency, so the tendency of our philanthropic and charitable agencies has been to pay no attention to the problem until it has expressed itself in terms of pauperism and delinquency. Such benevolence is not merely ineffectual; it is positively injurious to the community and to the future of the race.[11]

Sanger was especially derisive of private philanthropy and government interference assisting women during pregnancy. She warned:

> There is a special type of philanthropy or benevolence, now widely

advertised and advocated, both as a federal program and as worthy of private endowment, which strikes me as being more insidiously injurious than any other. This concerns itself directly with the function of maternity, and aims to supply free medical and nursing facilities to slum mothers. Such women are visited by nurses and receive instruction in the hygiene of pregnancy, and are guided in making arrangements for confinement; to be invited to come to the doctor's clinics for supervision.... Such benevolence is not merely superficial and nearsighted, it conceals a stupid cruelty, because it is not courageous enough to face unpleasant facts.... Such philanthropy encourages the healthier and more normal sections of the world to shoulder the burden of the unthinking and indiscriminate fecundity of others; which brings with it, as I think the reader must agree, a dead weight of human waste. Instead of decreasing and aiming to eliminate the stocks that are most detrimental to the future of the race and the world, it tends to render them to a menacing degree, dominant.[12]

While feminists have long contended that Sanger—now enthroned as a foremother of the women's movement—was a philanthropist who only wanted the best for women and children, her own writing and political activism show her to have been, in reality, an elitist who wanted poor women and children to be eliminated.

In the late 1930s, as the emerging Nazi movement took the commitment to eugenics to its logical extreme, Sanger tempered her rhetoric about "genetically inferior races." While Hitler was putting the quest for the Nietzschean Superman into practice in the extermination of the Jews, Sanger and her eugenicist comrades thought twice about their Social Darwinist convictions. Worried that a connection would be made between Hitler's now-unpopular eugenics and her own, Sanger changed her organization's name and rhetoric. "Birth control," with its undertone of coercion, became "family planning." The "unfit" and the "dysgenic" became merely "the poor." There was little talk of "cleansing the races" as the American Birth Control League morphed into the Planned Parenthood Federation of America.[13]

Michael Perry, editor of a collection of writings related to Sanger's *The Pivot of Civilization,* shows that Sanger and her associates merely shifted their rhetoric, not their basic philosophy. Perry points out that Sanger still returned to the strident, individualistic rhetoric of the Nietzschean Superman in front of certain audiences.

For her, members of the superior race could be free to live as they chose only if the inferior were kept from swamping the world with their tainted offspring. That distinction between superior and inferior humans lay at the heart of Sanger's worldview throughout her life and guided her life's work.[14]

Following her death in 1966, Planned Parenthood began distributing the "Maggie Awards," named after Sanger, to those who have made significant contributions to society in general and to women in particular. It is likely that most of those who have received these awards have little idea of what Sanger really believed. The Population Research Institute's president, Stephen Mosher, reminded everyone of the true Sanger legacy a few years ago in a *Wall Street Journal* op-ed. Mosher recalled that the first recipient of the Maggie Award was Martin Luther King Jr., who most likely was unaware that Sanger had "inaugurated a project to set his people free from their progeny." Mosher noted that Sanger had once written, "We do not want word to go out that we want to exterminate the Negro population and the Minister is the man who can straighten out that idea if it ever occurs to any of their more rebellious members." Mosher maintained that "had Dr. King known why he may have been chosen to receive the Maggie Award, he would have recoiled in horror."[15]

The dark side of the Sanger legacy continues today in the heavy marketing of abortion in the African American community. The fact that more than three-fourths of all abortion clinics are located within or adjacent to minority communities is not the only reason for the tremendous racial disparities in abortion rates, but it certainly is a contributing factor. Recent research by academic economists reveals that the increased availability of abortion services is itself a significant predictor of increased abortion within a given geographical area— even controlling for race and ethnicity. Using information from the Texas Department of Health, the economist Robert Brown analyzed the patterns of all births and abortions in the state for one year in relation to the availability or geographical proximity of abortion providers. He correlated data on completed abortions with the "travel costs" incurred by women seeking abortion. The results of this analysis suggested that pregnant women who reside in counties with longer travel distances to the nearest abortion provider have lower probabilities of aborting their pregnancies than women in counties closer to abortion providers. Mathematical simulations showed that changes in travel distance had a relatively large impact on overall abortion rates, and that the results varied by race. Brown found that when he compared overall rates of abortion for the women in his study, 20.2 percent of pregnancies among white women were aborted, 17.2 percent of pregnancies among Hispanic women were aborted, and 32.5 percent of pregnancies among black women. When comparisons were made by race and ethnicity, the data indicated that Latina women tended to live farther from abortion providers than did black women and were more affected by higher travel costs for abortion—and less likely to obtain an abortion than either white or black women.[16]

While there are many possible explanations for the correlation between accessibility of abortion providers and consumption of abortion services, the most obvious is economic: lower travel costs make abortion more affordable. But there are also far more important cultural reasons having to do with attitudinal or "push" factors that make abortion a more positive solution to an unplanned pregnancy. Greater availability of abortion services may decrease the stigma of such services, for instance, by signaling "social approval for the abortion decision"—or, in economic terms, by lowering "the psychic cost of terminating an unwanted pregnancy."[17] When an abortion clinic is located in the neighborhood, the residents are more likely to see it as just another neighborhood service. Once the culture of abortion is established in a neighborhood, the resistance of those who live there begins to break down.

In addition to attempting to plant a culture of abortion in African American neighborhoods, the pro-choice movement has renewed its effort during the past decade to locate abortion-services facilities in poor Hispanic neighborhoods in various states including California, Arizona, and Texas. In fact, Marcella Melendez, president of Hispanic Women for Life, claims that "there is a targeting of Hispanic women" by abortion providers. Melendez was referring to a report issued by the California Department of Health Services in 2000 on abortions paid for from public funds. The thirty-one-page report revealed that "abortion services to Latinas accounted for 34 percent of all fee-for-service abortions, exceeding the percentage of white females for the eighth consecutive year." In contrast, whites accounted for just 26 percent of all government-paid abortions, even though they make up a larger percentage of California's overall population. (The United States Census Bureau reports that whites account for 46.7 percent of all Californians; Hispanics 32.4 percent.) Abortions performed on "undocumented aliens" accounted for 15 percent of all government-paid abortions in California, which the report notes is 13 percent higher than the previous year. Altogether, 6,995 abortions were performed on "undocumented aliens" at tax-payer expense.[18]

Although California does not disseminate abortion data in general, it does release data from Medi-Cal because it is the state's social-welfare program. The Department of Health Services report demonstrated that Californians paid for 45,794 abortions directly covered by Medi-Cal. The state paid an average of $322 per abortion. An estimated 29,415 additional abortions were performed through managed-care affiliates of Medi-Cal, but there was no estimate of the cost in the report. Abortions performed for enrollees in health-care plans, otherwise known as managed care, are included in this report only as estimates, so we cannot say for sure how many abortions these plans provide. The only reliable numbers come from actual claims paid by Medi-Cal directly, and though limited in scope, they provide evidence of an obvious trend: in county after county, Hispanics make up a disproportionate share of women who have abortions paid for by the state. *San Diego News Notes,* a Catholic newspaper, documented that "in Fresno County, of the 1,588 Medi-Cal abortions, 289 or 18 percent were performed on white women, while 731 or 46 percent were performed on Hispanic women." The statistics were similar in other counties in the states with high Hispanic populations.[19]

Just as African American women have been targeted since the earliest days of the birth-control movement, Hispanic and Native American women are now viewed as likely consumers of abortion services. In interviews conducted at the March for Women's Lives in Washington, D.C., the *Chronicle of Higher Education* profiled a lesbian, Native American college student, Colette Denali Montoya-Humphrey, who served as a bus-trip organizer for Choice USA, a national nonprofit group that supports abortion rights. Montoya-

Humphrey said that she recruited more than 250 college students from Chicago, Madison, and Milwaukee for the March for Women's Lives. A student at the University of Wisconsin at Madison, Montoya-Humphrey, who is a member of the Isleta and San Felipe Pueblo tribes, said she "made an effort to recruit minority women and lesbians for the march.... Choice is not just about safe and legal abortions, it is about ensuring access to reproductive health care for all women regardless of their background, especially women of color, queer women, people with disabilities, and low income people." Wearing a bright orange Choice USA T-shirt, Montoya-Humphrey said that she had written "American Indian, Catholic, Queer on the back of her shirt to 'show solidarity' with her people."[20]

From the earliest days of the reproductive-rights movement led by Sanger, there was an attempt to broaden what was then a radical idea of birth control beyond its socialist and feminist roots. The book jacket of the recent reissue of *The Pivot of Civilization* approvingly remarks:

> Shifting the focus from women's reproductive rights to the larger issue of the general welfare of the whole human race, Sanger argues that birth control is pivotal to a rational approach toward dealing with the threat of overpopulation and its ruinous consequences in poverty and disease.... While critics on both the right and the left have sought to diminish Sanger's achievements, based on the context of her arguments, they can never obscure her powerful feminist message: when women gain greater control over their fertility they will improve the human race.[21]

Today there are similar attempts to demonstrate the value of abortion to society, far beyond serving the needs of individuals directly involved in the abortion itself. Professors John Donohue and Steven Levitt of the University of California at Berkeley recently provided a powerful economic argument in favor of abortion that relies on many of the stereotypes first promoted by the eugenicists of the Sanger era. In a paper entitled "The Impact of Legalized Abortion on Crime," Donohue and Levitt use elaborate mathematical models to marshal evidence that legalized abortion has contributed significantly to crime reductions. They maintain that crime began to fall roughly eighteen years after abortion was legalized, and point out that the five states that allowed abortion in 1970 experienced declines earlier than the rest of the nation, which legalized it in 1973 with *Roe v. Wade*. States with high abortion rates in the 1970s and 1980s experienced greater crime reductions in the 1990s, according to the authors. They contend that "legalized abortion appears to account for as much as 50 percent of the drop in crime."[22]

Donohue and Levitt write that the "smaller cohort that results from abortion legalization means that when that cohort reaches the late teens and twenties, there will be fewer young males in their highest crime years and thus, less crime." They deduce that the aborted children would have been more likely than average to become criminals, both because of their mothers' demographic characteristics, disproportionately black or Hispanic, young and poor, and because of the children's "unwantedness."

Directly addressing the effects of race and abortion on crime rates, Donohue and Levitt conclude that more abortions by African American women will result in fewer homicides for society. The Berkeley professors claim:

> [G]iven that homicide rates of black youths are roughly nine times higher than those of white youths, racial differences in the fertility effects of abortion are likely to translate into greater homicide reductions. Under the assumption that those black and white births eliminated by legalized abortion would have experienced the average criminal propensities of their respective races, then the predicted reduction in homicide is 8.9 percent. In other words, taking into account differential abortion rates by race raises the predicted impact of abortion legalization on homicide from 5.4 percent to 8.9 percent.[23]

In the spirit of Sanger, Professors Donohue and Levitt say their data demonstrate that abortion is the strongest contributor to the reduction in crime rates in society. They believe that higher rates of incarceration, improved policing strategies, and a decline in the crack cocaine industry on the streets may have contributed somewhat to the decrease, but their statistical models indicate that legalized abortion is the primary explanation for the large drops in murder, property crime, and violent crime that our nation has experienced over the last decade. In fact, they claim that "the social benefit to reduced crime as a result of abortion may be on the order of $30 billion annually." And they predict that, "all else being equal, legalized abortion will account for persistent declines of 1 percent per year over the next two decades." The authors warn, however, that continued crime reduction in the future will depend on unlimited access to abortion, especially for the poor. In fact, they predict that any attempts to limit abortion will result in higher crime rates, and they subtly offer suggestions for public policy: "To the extent that the Hyde Amendment effectively restricts access to abortion by denying Medicaid funds to the poor for abortion, this prediction [of lower crime rates] might be overly optimistic."[24]

Provocative though this argument may be, there are reasons to question the abortion-crime link. As Ramesh Ponnuru recently pointed out in an opinion piece in the *Wall Street Journal,* Britain's crime rate was rising twenty years after abortion was legalized. (Ponnuru also suggests that "It is possible, also, that the legalization of abortion increased crime by undermining respect for the sanctity of life, although any such effect would be hard to measure.")[25] Russians abort seven out of ten pregnancies and their society is more dangerous than ever. In a recent monograph on the underclass for the American Enterprise Institute, Charles Murray contends that while crime is falling, the number of criminals in America is actually still rising—which suggests that crime is dropping not because there are fewer offenders but mainly because more of them are behind bars.

Donohue and Levitt were criticized by the pro-life community when their study was first released in 1999, although they never overtly advocated a higher abortion rate as a way to address the crime problem. In fact, Levitt teamed up with a new co-author, Stephen Dubner, to write about a number of interesting economic questions "from cheating and crime to sports and childrearing" in a recent best-selling book, *Freakonomics,* which looked again at the relationship between abortion and crime. While avoiding the issue of how increased African American abortion rates bear on crime reduction, *Freakonomics* does acknowledge that an economic calculation of benefits that abortion may yield in terms of crime rates can be unsettling for some readers. In an apparent nod to his pro-life critics, Levitt recalls his response to first realizing that abortion appeared to be the major contributor to crime reduction: "To discover that abortion was one of the greatest crime-lowering factors in American history is, needless to say, jarring. It feels less Darwinian than Swiftian; it calls to mind a long ago dart attributed to G. K. Chesterton: when there aren't enough hats to go around, the problem isn't solved by lopping off some heads." The crime drop was, in the language of economists, an "unintended benefit" of legalized abortion. But Levitt admits, "one need not oppose abortion on moral or religious grounds to feel shaken by the notion of a private sadness being converted into a public good."[26]

CHAPTER THREE

Inside Abortion
inside Washington

IN THE FIRST WEEK of his first term as presi-
dent, symbolically scheduling the event on January 22, 1993, to
commemorate the twentieth anniversary of *Roe v. Wade,* Bill Clinton abruptly terminated five federal pro-life policies, beginning with
the ban on abortion counseling at federally funded Title X clinics.[1]
Targeting these clinics appears to have been a calculated decision by
the Clinton administration to address what the president's supporters viewed as inadequate access to abortion for the poor. In 1970,
Congress had enacted Title X of the Public Health Service Act to
give millions of poor and low-income women access to reproductive-
health services that they otherwise could not afford. But under
President Reagan in 1988, regulations were issued that prohibited
these federally funded family-planning clinics from informing their
patients about abortion. Called the "Gag Rule" by pro-choice advocates, the regulations prevented these clinics from referring pregnant
women to abortion providers. Instead of abortion referrals, federally funded clinics were required to give their pregnant patients a
referral list of health-care providers that promoted the welfare of
mother and unborn child, not including those that offered abortion
as their principal service. All of these restrictions ended in the first
week of the Clinton presidency.

Lauding President Clinton's decisions in her book *Killing the Black Body,* Dorothy Roberts, an African American law professor, decried the fact that prior to Clinton's "intervention," counseling about the availability of abortion services had been "unfairly denied to Black women." Ignoring the significant racial disparities in abortion rates and the fact that three-fourths of all abortion facilities are housed in minority neighborhoods, Roberts asserted that because of a lack of information about where they could obtain abortions, many black women were "unaware of their right to an abortion... and often turn to newspaper ads that can steer them in a dangerous direction."[2]

Roberts was not alone in her enthusiasm for the new policies of the Clinton administration. Other abortion proponents viewed these sweeping pro-abortion reforms as a kind of Emancipation Proclamation for women. Eleanor Smeal of the Feminist Majority said they marked "the end of an era" of pro-life tyranny. NARAL's Kate Michelman declared, "We have turned the corner to a new day for choice in America." The *Washington Post* and the *Boston Globe* both proclaimed "a new era of pro-choice supremacy." And the *New York Times* announced, "The Abortion Tide Turns."[3]

Optimism about a new "abortion era" was realized when reports surfaced that President Clinton had omitted the Hyde amendment from his first proposed budget. Enacted in 1977, the Hyde amendment was a yearly Medicaid rider that ended most federal involvement in subsidizing abortion services and instead relegated that role to the states. Under the Hyde amendment, Medicaid pays for abortion only when the woman's life is endangered by her pregnancy. The amendment has had great popular appeal for voters, and as a result, Congress has renewed it every year since 1977. But because it is a "yearly rider," the Clinton administration's omission of the Hyde amendment from its budget proposal was significant. Clinton spokesman George Stephanopoulos explained, "the President feels that Hyde goes too far."[4] Maintaining that Clinton's real concern was "to preserve the flexibility of the states in administering Medicaid," Stephanopoulos said that Clinton only wanted to "create equal access to abortion" for all women, including the poor. The idea that President Clinton wanted only to preserve states' rights in abortion decisions gave insiders a smile, since at the same time as his administration was attempting to repeal the Hyde amendment, Clinton was also endorsing the Freedom of Choice Act, which would prohibit states from limiting abortion even if *Roe v. Wade* were some day overturned.

The dangers in repealing Hyde and in passing the Freedom of Choice Act were clear, even to moderates on the abortion issue. As a result, opposition to Clinton's plans for increasing federal funding for abortion grew quickly. In response to the administration's dramatic pro-abortion policy decisions and the publicity surrounding the abortion provisions of its National Health Security Plan, the Christian Coalition purchased a full-page ad in the *Washington Post* of April 22, 1993, denouncing the new movement toward taxpayer support of abortion. The ad included a copy of the 1987 letter in which Al Gore had pronounced his opposition to federal financing of abortion, with the headline: "Al Gore Was Right." The Christian Coalition's ad claimed that a CBS News/ *New York Times* poll showed that 72 percent of all American people opposed taxpayer-funded abortion.[5]

It was not only evangelical Christians who were concerned. In a column in *U.S. News & World Report,* the political strategist David Gergen cautioned Clinton against "opening the floodgates to universal abortion on demand, funded by taxpayers." Instead, Gergen praised the example of President Carter, who had supported the Hyde amendment "on the sensible premise that the government should stay out of a woman's decision, not blocking her but not encouraging her either."[6] Validating such a cautious view, at the end of June 1993 the House of Representatives voted 255 to 178 to renew the Hyde amendment. Even some new members of the House who had been elected the previous November with generous financial support from pro-choice advocacy groups voted for the amendment. Seeing that the majority of their constituents would not appreciate their tax dollars being devoted to the delivery of abortion services, supporters of the Freedom of Choice Act gave up any hope of its passage, and in September 1993 the Senate renewed the Hyde amendment for yet another year.

When President and Mrs. Clinton revealed their national health-care plan a few months later, few were surprised to learn that the plan mandated payment for abortion services as a "medically necessary health care service" to be included as part of the basic benefits package. While the Clintons' National Health Security Plan would have replaced all existing health insurance with a plan that included abortion as a basic benefit, it also replaced the word "abortion" with the euphemistic phrase "medically necessary reproductive health services."

Although leaders of pro-choice advocacy organizations like Planned Parenthood, NARAL Pro-Choice America, and Catholics for a Free Choice applauded the Clinton plan, the response from representatives of the more conservative religious denominations was overwhelmingly negative. In fact, three religious pro-life groups, representing the Catholic, Lutheran, and Southern Baptist faiths, publicly condemned the plan. A leader from Lutherans for Life went so far as to decry the health-care plan as a means of facilitating "evil" because of its requirement that millions of citizens violate their consciences by paying for abortion.[7]

Some of these religious leaders brought their concerns to their congregations and encouraged them to contact lawmakers in Washington. Cardinal Roger Mahoney, archbishop of Los Angeles and chairman of the National Conference of Catholic Bishops' Committee for Pro-Life Activities, urged Catholics to participate in a message campaign to Congress on January 23, 1994. "No government has the right to force us to finance the deliberate destruction of human lives," Mahoney wrote.[8]

Similarly, Richard D. Land, executive director of the Christian Life Commission of the Southern Baptist Convention, wrote that he "felt a responsibility to address the health care issue because President Clinton is a member of a Southern Baptist congregation and many Southern Baptists are deeply opposed to the President's agenda on human life issues." Land proposed a consultation on health-care reform in 1994 and said that "the inclusion of abortion on demand must be prevented." Land promised that "the Christian Life Commission will educate and involve grassroots Southern Baptists in this critical battle like we never have before on any other issue. We must not fail."[9] Representatives from Lutherans for Life issued a letter-writing "call to action" campaign to Lutheran congregations. Edward Feshkens, the organization's executive director, stated: "The witness of the Church for nearly two thousand years has consistently condemned the destruction of unborn human life by abortion. A nationally enforced, tax-payer funded regime of abortion will result in countless more deaths. Such a regime will also force millions of citizens to violate their consciences, compelling them to participate in that which is evil."[10]

Mrs. Clinton's proposal for national health insurance, including funding for abortion on demand to all women, eventually became—like the president's attempt to repeal the Hyde amendment—an early Clinton-administration casualty. But the president made abortion even more accessible later in his term. On two separate occasions, President Clinton used his veto to end legislation that would have banned an especially gruesome form of late-term abortion, more commonly known as partial-birth abortion. In an effort to expand abortion services, the president also ordered U.S. military facilities to provide abortions to servicewomen and resumed funding to the United Nations Family Planning Administration, which participates in the management of China's forced-abortion program. Clinton restored funding to pro-abortion organizations in foreign nations by declaring abortion to be a "fundamental right," and worked with representatives to the UN to establish an "international right" to abortion for all women. Clinton also encouraged his appointees to facilitate the introduction of the abortifacient RU-486 in the United States.

What the Clintons did not anticipate was that some people essentially on their side of the abortion wars were reluctant to support taxpayer-funded abortion. Their principled opposition to federal funding for abortion was grounded in the very real fear that any federal financial support for abortion might be construed as implied coercion to increase the abortion rate of poor women. Others from the pro-choice side decried the use of taxpayer dollars to fund abortion as just one more instance of the "out-of-control" welfare services to the poor. These more pragmatic pro-choice advocates argued that although they, too, supported a woman's right to choose, taxpayers should not be forced to pay for the abortions of poor women receiving Medicaid. This libertarian-leaning contingent was successful in bringing its argument directly to those with an interest in lower taxes and smaller government. Some pro-life advocates even joined this group in an attempt to broaden the appeal of the pro-life position by creating a more pragmatic or utilitarian argument against abortion funding. Eventually, these forces converged to help bring the most sweeping reform of the welfare system since its creation more than sixty years earlier.

Welfare reform transferred primary responsibility for aid to families with children away from the federal government to the states, and it encouraged the poor to make the transition from dependency to self-sufficiency by requiring states to meet specific timetables for putting welfare recipients to work. But, more importantly with regard to reproductive decisions, the 1995 welfare-reform law committed nearly $850 million in public funds to promote abstinence and to reward states that reduce out-of-wedlock births and abortions among all women in each state. During their first year in power, members of the 1994 Congress barred federal employees' health insurance from covering abortions. They outlawed the use of American military hospitals for abortion on U.S. servicewomen and dependents of soldiers stationed abroad. They banned federal funding of abortion for federal prisoners. And they eliminated 35 percent of U.S. aid to international family-planning programs.[11]

In an attempt to reduce the number of out-of-wedlock pregnancies and encourage the formation of two-parent families, welfare-reform provisions allowed states to use block-grant funds for programs designed to end the dependence of the poor on government benefits by promoting job preparation, work, and marriage; to reduce the incidence of out-of-wedlock pregnancies and establish annual numerical goals for decreasing the numbers of these pregnancies; and, finally, to provide assistance to needy families so that children may be cared for in their own homes or by relatives.[12]

In order to create an incentive for states to lower the incidence of out-of-wedlock childbearing without increasing the rate of abortion, those designing the welfare-reform legislation included what became known as the "illegitimacy bonus." Reformers passed a proposal that in each of four years beginning in 1999, the five states that achieved the greatest decreases in out-of-wedlock births among all women, not just welfare recipients or teenagers, and also reduced their abortion rates below the level in 1995 would receive $20 million each. If fewer than five states qualified, each state would receive $25 million.[13]

While the "process issues" related to the illegitimacy bonus presented challenges, it is the complex data-collection issues that have made it almost unworkable in practice. While most states collect and report data on abortions to the Centers for Disease Control and Prevention (CDC), some report 35 to 50 percent fewer abortions than the state's abortion providers say they are performing. The Alan Guttmacher Institute has much more reliable information because it collects data directly from abortion providers, and these figures indicate much higher rates of abortion than do the CDC statistics. Worse, five states do not even collect abortion statistics at all. (Among these is California, which accounts for 12 percent of the U.S. population.) The CDC estimates data from these states with varying degrees of reliability. As the Guttmacher Institute points out, "Whether these states would be eligible to compete for the illegitimacy bonus is not clear. If they are not, some are likely to challenge their ineligibility in court. But, if they are deemed eligible and any win a bonus, the award may be disputed by states that actually report abortion data."[14]

Beyond the problems inherent in implementing and evaluating the effectiveness of the illegitimacy bonus, one of the most controversial components of the welfare-reform proposal focused on what became known as the "family cap." Also called the child-exclusion provision, the family cap was a proposal to deny increased cash payments to a woman who conceives and bears another child while she is receiving welfare. Had it been passed by Congress, this proposal would have "capped" payments to the woman at the level of funding the family was given when they first applied for welfare. For example, if a woman had two children at that time but gave birth to twins three weeks later, she would receive support only for the original two children.

Some anti-abortion advocates, including religious leaders, argued that the family cap would result in more abortions among welfare recipients, as there would no longer be an economic incentive to carry a child to term. As a result, the family-cap proposal met opposition from three strange bedfellows, including pro-life advocates and pro-choice advocates along with welfare-rights advocates. While the pro-lifers worried that the family cap would cause an increase in abortion on the part of mothers who could not afford to have another child, pro-choicers maintained that the family-cap program would be ineffective in influencing birth rates and would put an undue burden on women. Welfare-rights advocates had little interest in the ideological issues surrounding abortion and claimed that their only concern was over an increased rate of poverty among women.[15]

For the first time, pro-life and pro-choice advocates were united, as both sides believed the reform would be harmful to poor women and children. Their opposition to the family cap paid off as the child-exclusion provisions were deleted from the federal welfare-reform bill and states were given the option to craft their own family-cap legislation. By 1998, a total of twenty-three states had implemented family-cap or child-exclusion provisions. But giving states this right drew an angry response from some pro-life conservative members of Congress.

Representative Christopher H. Smith of New Jersey argued that "the family cap is likely to tip the balance for each poor woman who feels that society has no real interest in the survival of her baby." Under such a provision, he warned, the mother "will get a powerfully negative message—that her child has no value—especially from those states where Medicaid abortion is readily available." He predicted that with a family cap in place, "one of two things will happen: either the woman will have an abortion, or the family will descend further into poverty." Representative Smith introduced new legislation that would have barred states from applying their own version of a family cap and thus "punishing" women for having additional children: he proposed that the federal government block Temporary Assistance to Needy Families (TANF) grants to any states that enacted a family cap. Smith pointed out that since the family cap had been implemented in New Jersey in 1993, more than nine hundred abortions had occurred there on account of the law. He also argued that "thousands of other children have also been left to fend for themselves because their parents were not allowed to receive assistance on their behalf."[16]

While intuitively appealing, the evidence that Smith cited as "proof" of the problems with the family-cap provisions was a deeply flawed preliminary draft of a study by professors at Rutgers University. Conducted by Michael Camasso of the Rutgers Department of Social Work, the study found that the abortion rate in New

Jersey had not declined as much as trend data would have predicted it should as a result of the welfare reform—and from this trend data, Camasso concluded that the abortion rate had "increased." According to Camasso, the predicted decline had not occurred because women were "forced" to have abortions out of increased economic hardship. The problem was that the Camasso study was later described by sociologists as "so flawed" that it could never have been used to inform policy decisions.[17]

Still, as soon as the first recipients had begun to be affected by the family-cap provisions and the Rutgers preliminary data were released, appearing to confirm their worst fears on abortion "increases," opponents filed lawsuits in an attempt to overturn the family caps. The earliest lawsuits were unsuccessful because they relied on the novel argument that the reform was an experiment and therefore women should have to give informed consent before being subjected to the family-cap provisions. But judges ruled that federal law explicitly exempts this kind of change in benefit programs from informed-consent provisions. The opponents, however, reserved the right to bring a lawsuit in New Jersey state courts, arguing that the reform violated privacy rights inherent in the state constitution. Drawing from the Camasso preliminary data, the later lawsuits have centered on the allegation that the abortion rate had increased as a result of the reform.[18]

A follow-up study by the sociologists Peter Rossi of the University of Massachusetts and Ted Goertzel of Rutgers disputed the Camasso findings because "there were serious problems with the integrity of the implementation of the experimental design which made those results less than definitive." Rossi and Goertzel found that, in contrast to the preliminary study by Camasso, "time series research showed that trends in New Jersey were quite favorable to the reform: welfare case loads and births to welfare mothers were down. Indicators of child welfare, such as infant mortality and low birth rate infants, were positive." And, most importantly, Rossi and Goertzel testified that the follow-up data on abortion rates revealed no increase resulting from the family cap; rather, abortion rates in New Jersey had actually continued to decline.[19]

Realizing the futility of attempting to "predict" what the abortion rates might have been had the family caps not been implemented, the New Jersey Department of Human Services discontinued the Camasso evaluation of the state's family-cap program. Besides, the "welfare to work" reforms driven by a Republican-led Congress in 1996 had changed conditions for families so much that studies of the effects of family caps were no longer relevant. The reforms had given states greater authority to run their own welfare programs. After 1996, states were given the power to deny welfare to any child whose unmarried teenage mother failed to stay in school and live with an adult. Congress also gave states the ability to compete for the illegitimacy bonus—with the caveat that any increase in abortion rates would penalize them. The family cap remained an option for states to implement if they chose to do so.[20] But federal law established a lifetime limit of five years for payments to any family and required family heads to find a job within two years. Welfare reform so dramatically improved the lives of most women, because of their transition from welfare to work, that most of the legal challenges to the family cap are moot.

Despite the intramural fights throughout the Clinton years, there had been far less concern about the effects of welfare reform than there were in the earliest days of the George W. Bush administration, when, as Brent Bozell of the Media Research Center remarked, "You can tell a Republican lives in the White House now because the media has rediscovered poverty and homelessness." But it was the Democrats who "rediscovered" abortion and claimed that it had increased because of Republican social policies. On January 24, 2005, Hillary Clinton decried the "fact" that abortion was increasing under the Bush administration: "Unfortunately in the last few years, while we are engaged in an ideological debate instead of one that uses facts and evidence and common sense, the rate of abortion is on the rise in some states. In the three years since President Bush took office, eight states saw an increase in abortion, a 14.6 percent average increase, and four states saw a decrease (4.3 percent average), so we have a lot of work still ahead of us."[21]

A few days later, in an interview on NBC's *Meet the Press,* Senator John Kerry also claimed that abortions had increased. Kerry asked the host, Tim Russert, "Do you know that in fact abortion has gone up in these last few years with the draconian policies that Republicans have put into place?" And on May 22, 2005, in what was the strangest of these assertions, Howard Dean, the Democratic National Committee chairman, said on *Meet the Press* that "abortions have gone up 25 percent since George W. Bush was named President."[22]

It was an ingenious ploy to confuse the abortion debate as it had traditionally been framed in Washington, but the truth is that abortions have actually decreased under President George W. Bush's administration. The Alan Guttmacher Institute reported that the number of abortions declined by 0.8 percent in 2001 and again by 0.8 percent in 2002. (The Guttmacher Institute, certainly no supporter of the Bush administration, was founded in 1968 in honor of a former president of the Planned Parenthood Federation of America and describes its mission as being to "protect reproductive choice of all women and men in the United States and throughout the world.") The institute's data indicate that abortion rates under Bush have followed an ongoing pattern of decline.[23]

The abortion rate in the United States peaked in 1980, and after 1990 it declined substantially, so that by 2000 it was at the lowest level since 1974. Guttmacher estimated that the number of abortions performed in the United States in 2001 was 1,303,000. This represents a decline of 0.8 percent from the 1,313,000 abortions performed in 2000. The number of abortions declined again in 2002, to 1,293,000. Guttmacher also estimated that 21.1 of every 1,000 women ages 15 to 44 had an abortion in 2001. This figure represents a decline of 0.2 points or 1 percent from the 2000 rate of 21.3. The 2002 abortion rate was 20.9, down 0.2 points or 0.9 percent from the previous year.[24] The Guttmacher study points out that reasons for changes in the abortion rate are hard to determine without placing the data in a broader context. They note that these trend estimates are averages for the whole country and remind readers that it is likely there are significant variations from the national trend within individual states and within particular population subgroups. Most importantly, however, the Guttmacher researchers indicate that while the abortion rate declined among most groups between 1994 and 2000, it increased among poor women and women receiving Medicaid.[25]

This increase in abortion rates for poor and minority women was not widely reported in the media, perhaps because it occurred during the Clinton administration. Even Mrs. Clinton appears to have forgotten about the "sad" statistics on rising rates of abortion for poor, black, and Hispanic women. She also neglected to mention in her 2005 statement that although abortion rates have been declining since 1990, the decline was strongest in the first half of the decade, which began with George H. W. Bush in office, but actually slowed during President Clinton's term and even reversed itself in one year.[26]

How did Hillary Clinton, John Kerry, and Howard Dean get these statistics on abortion rates under the Bush administration so wrong? And where could Howard Dean have gotten the statistic of a 25 percent increase in abortions? The nonpartisan Annenberg Political Fact Check (FactCheck.org) has tried to find out. In an article entitled "The Biography of a Bad Statistic," FactCheck published the dubious origins of the Clinton, Kerry, and Dean "statistics" and wrote: "We asked the Democratic National Committee repeatedly to tell us where Dean got his 25 percent figure, but we got no response." It would appear that Howard Dean simply made it up. And, since NBC host Tim Russert left the statistic unchallenged, millions of *Meet the Press* viewers assumed that the statistic was true. No one, including Russert, has ever corrected Dean's false assertion.

To be fair to John Kerry and Hillary Clinton, however, FactCheck found that in their more modest claim of an abortion upsurge, both Democratic leaders had relied upon data, albeit faulty, contained in an obscure (and seriously flawed) opinion piece published in the *Houston Chronicle* and posted on the Internet. The authors, Glen Harold Stassen, an ethics professor at Fuller Theological Seminary, and Gary Krane, a self-described "independent investigative journalist" in Philadelphia, published the piece entitled "Why Abortion Rate Is Up in Bush Years" on October 17, 2004— just in time for the November presidential elections. Stassen and Krane alleged that Kentucky's abortion rate increased by 3.2 percent from 2000 to 2003; Michigan's by 11.3 percent; Pennsylvania's by 1.9 percent; and Colorado's by an astounding 111 percent. Stassen and Krane also claimed to have found that of the twelve additional states that reported statistics for 2001 and 2002, eight saw an increase in abortion rates (14.6 percent average increase) and four saw a decrease (4.3 percent average).[27]

Stassen and Krane, both Kerry supporters, blamed this alleged rise in abortion on Bush economic policies. But while there was little time to rebut their assertions before the presidential election, Guttmacher data later demonstrated how fatally flawed the Stassen and Krane study was.[28] While seven of the sixteen states that Stassen chose to measure abortion rates had small short-term fluctuations, they are not sufficient to establish a trend. Worse, many of the remaining states' data are just wrong. While Stassen said abortions in Wisconsin increased by 0.6 percent from 2001 to 2002, data from the Wisconsin Department of Health and Family Services indicate that there were actually 436 fewer abortions performed in Wisconsin in 2002 than in 2001. Likewise, although Stassen said abortions in South Dakota increased, the truth is that the state health agency's data for that period show a decrease of 9.7 percent. The large increases that Stassen cited for four of the sixteen states (including Colorado's alarming 111 percent increase) and the much smaller increases in Arizona, Idaho, and Michigan all raise other questions. According to Lifenews.com contributors Randy O'Bannon and Laura Hussey, "There is reason to believe that these may be unrepresentative aberrations attributable to changes in the gathering of statistics rather than to massive behavioral changes."[29] This certainly appears to be the case in Colorado.

Beyond the statistical problems in the Stassen and Krane article, there are even more serious problems related to Stassen's attempt to appeal to the pro-life community by representing himself as "consistently pro-life." In making the argument that other pro-life voters like himself would do better voting for Kerry, the pro-choice candidate, in order to reduce the number of abortions, Stassen neglected to mention that he had been a longtime activist in the pro-choice movement. While identifying himself as pro-life, Stassen left out the fact that he was one of the original signers of *A Call to Concern,* a 1977 document that expressed support for the *Roe v. Wade* decision, criticized the "absolutist" position of the Catholic Church, and affirmed that "abortion may be the most loving act possible." Even in the twisting road of abortion debate in Washington, his turn was abrupt and inexplicable.

CHAPTER FOUR

The Personal Is Political

WHILE MOST OF US would never think of ourselves as being involved in a "war" over abortion, we would still have to admit to taking sides on this contentious issue. Poll data reveal that there are few people without an opinion on either the right to abortion or the morality of the act. And although the major battles are being fought by people at the extremes of the pro-life and pro-choice positions, most of us are somewhere in the middle. There may be some common ground for the moderates on the pro-life and pro-choice sides—on the matter of federal funding, for instance, or parental permission for abortions on minor children— but the real warriors in this culture war hold such dramatically different philosophical, religious, and scientific positions that compromise is impossible.

While those on the pro-choice side believe they are defending a woman's right to end a pregnancy that has brought only sadness and pain and could negatively impact her chances for a fulfilling life, those on the pro-life side view themselves as defending not just a fetus but an unborn child with all the human potential and natural rights of a child carried to term. As the debate became ever more polarized in the 1980s and 1990s, the fanatical wing of the anti-abortion movement began to attract zealots ready to commit acts

of violence. Appropriating the language of war and driven by a dis-
torted view of Christianity, the Army of God and other groups within
this radical fringe engaged in abortion-clinic bombings and shootings in the same way that al-Qaeda terrorists kill in the name of a
twisted form of Islam. And, like the al-Qaeda directives and training
videos, the Army of God has published an anarchist's handbook with
detailed instructions on sabotaging abortion clinics, using silencers
for guns, and the assembly of explosive devices. Warning that "we are
forced to take aim against you...execution is rarely gentle," the Army
of God, the most extreme of the extremist groups affiliated with the
anti-abortion movement, continues even today to promote violence
against abortion providers.[1]

While there had been arson attacks and bombings at abortion
clinics in the 1980s, and even a kidnapping and release of a Florida
abortion provider in 1982 by anti-abortion zealots, it was not until
the spring of 1993 that the radical wing of the anti-abortion movement began the shooting war. Dr. David Gunn, an abortion provider
in Pensacola, Florida, became the first victim of a cluster of abortion-
provider shootings when Michael Griffin, a member of an extremist
anti-abortion group and sometime sidewalk protester outside abortion clinics, shot him in an effort to "move beyond the rhetoric of
the anti-abortion movement." In an interview with *Newsweek* writers
James Risen and Judy Thomas, Griffin recalled that on the morning
of March 5, 1993, he had driven into a Pensacola Exxon station
and, quite by chance, saw Dr. Gunn purchasing gasoline. "It was
Providence," Griffin told Risen and Thomas. Interpreting the
encounter as "a message from God," he had walked over to Gunn's
car at the gas pump and tapped on the window. "I looked him right
in the face and said, 'David Gunn, the Lord told me to tell you that
you have one more chance.'"[2] Five days later, Griffin shot Dr. Gunn
twice in the back as he walked from his car in the parking lot toward
his office at the Pensacola Women's Medical Services abortion clinic.
Griffin immediately turned himself in to a police officer, saying, "I
just shot Dr. Gunn."[3]

In his defense, Griffin's lawyers claimed that their client had
been "brainwashed" into committing the murder by the leaders of a
militant anti-abortion group. His attorneys described the "relent-
less rhetoric and graphic images" shown to him by a longtime

Pensacola anti-abortion leader, John Burt. The *New York Times* reported that "the campaign included videos, books, prayer sessions, the use of an effigy of Dr. Gunn and even a funeral for an aborted fetus."[4] Although Griffin was convicted and given a life sentence, he achieved hero status within the fringe groups like Army of God. In fact, the Southern Poverty Law Center's Intelligence Report has published the names of those individuals who signed the 1993 "defensive action statement" in support of Griffin and his murderous act. This statement has become well known within the radical anti-abortion movement as one of the definitive lists identifying those who view the killing of abortion doctors as "justifiable homicide":

> We the undersigned, declare the justice of taking all godly action necessary to defend innocent human life including the use of force. We proclaim that whatever force is legitimate to defend the life of a born child is legitimate to defend the life of an unborn child. We assert that if Michael Griffin did in fact kill Dr. David Gunn, his use of lethal force was justifiable provided it was carried out for the purpose of defending the lives of unborn children.[5]

As James Davison Hunter predicted in his 1994 book about the culture wars, *Before the Shooting Begins,* others soon began to emulate Griffin. Within a few months, Dr. George Tiller, an abortion provider in Wichita, Kansas, was shot and slightly wounded in the arm by Rachelle Shannon, an anti-abortion activist from southern Oregon. Describing herself as "a soldier" in the journal entries she posted on the Army of God website, Shannon was also a member of Advocates for Life and Lambs of Christ, but said that she felt it necessary to do "something more meaningful" than blocking clinic entrances and doing sidewalk counseling. In a computer file labeled "Mom's Jail Time Total," she described her time in jail as "the price she paid for being a soldier dedicated to rescuing babies." Shannon proudly documented her activities and her "punishment" of ninety-eight days. Then, sometime in 1991, she decided that she had to up the ante.[6]

In a document entitled "Join the Army," Shannon wrote: "The biggest hurdle was being willing to even consider that God could actually require this work of anyone.... Christians don't do that kind of thing, do they? But, prayer and God cleared that up. Then I

realized that I needed to stop the baby-killing too."⁷ Recalling what
she viewed as Giffin's "heroic deed" in killing Dr. Gunn, and in an
effort to prepare for the escalation of her own anti-abortion activities, Shannon exchanged letters with "courageous" men and women
jailed for their actions "on behalf of the babies." Finding names and
addresses of like-minded militants on the "Prisoners of Christ" website, Shannon began to question why more of her "comrades in arms
didn't seem to realize that babies were being murdered and therefore
see the need to stop the holocaust."

Eventually, Rachelle Shannon began to distance herself from
pro-lifers she regarded as unwilling to "put it all on the line" or
"pay the price." In her journals, she recalled that she had "participated in her last blockade on November 17, 1992," and then
committed herself to doing the "real work to stop the killing of the
innocent" any way she could. She believed it was a "sign" from God
to go ahead with her plan when a five-gallon gas can "miraculously"
appeared in her garage. It did not matter that her husband had inno-
cently brought the gas can home from work, where it was about to
be thrown into the trash. In Shannon's view, the arson materials
had been sent directly from God. She succeeded in her first attempt
at starting a fire at an abortion facility in Ashland, Oregon, and then
moved on to an abortion clinic in Reno, Nevada, where she posed
as a patient in need of services. Once there, she released a canister
of butyric acid, a caustic, foul-smelling chemical that rendered the
abortion facility uninhabitable for weeks. In November 1992, she
firebombed an abortion clinic in Alhambra, California. But once
she heard that Griffin had shot Dr. Gunn in 1993, she felt that "her
course of action was clear." Finding biblical support for her deadly
plans, Shannon wrote: "Like Phehas and Jael and even Samuel of the
Bible, the righteous thing to do was to meet deadly force with
equally deadly force."⁸

After obtaining a .25 caliber pistol from a friend, Shannon prepared to kill Dr. George Tiller. She chose Tiller for what she called "a
termination" because she viewed the "late term abortionist" as the
most "notorious" abortion provider in the country. Tiller was not
seriously wounded in her attack, however, and actually was able to
follow her car as she raced away from the parking lot of the abortion facility. Arrested and convicted of attempted murder, Shannon

was sentenced to eleven years in prison. Later, extradited back to Oregon to stand trial for a series of abortion-clinic bombings there, she was convicted and sentenced to an additional twenty years in prison.

The Army of God still describes Rachelle Shannon as "a good soldier" because of her unwillingness to incriminate any other anti-abortion leaders. She continued her anti-abortion writings in prison; her 1994 Christmas letter described the "good news" for her cause: "For the Army of God, 1994 was a great year. We had another termination procedure on an abortionist and his accomplice and [the killer] may be put to death for his obedience to God. This is a most honorable way for a Christian to die."

In 1994, the shooting war had moved back to Pensacola, where Paul Hill, a former Presbyterian minister and leader of the anti-abortion group Defensive Action, joined the other "heroes" in the extremist movement. Emulating Michael Griffin, Hill shot and killed Dr. John Britton, an abortion provider, and fatally wounded James H. Barrett, a retired Air Force colonel who was serving as an escort for clinic personnel and women entering the Pensacola clinic. Hill, who also critically wounded Barrett's wife with the twelve-gauge shotgun he carried to the parking lot of the abortion clinic, had recently become involved in the same kind of pro-life activism and sidewalk counseling in Pensacola as Michael Griffin. In fact, following the killing of David Gunn, Hill telephoned the producers of *The Phil Donohue Show* to say that he supported Griffin's actions. A few days later, Phil Donohue invited Hill to appear on his show to discuss the killing with Dr. Gunn's son. The televised appearance provided an opportunity for Hill to compare the killing of Dr. Gunn to the killing of Nazi concentration-camp doctors, and he quickly became a hero to the fanatical wing of the anti-abortion advocacy movement.[9] Paul Hill became a martyr after his execution by the State of Florida. Even today, years later, his picture and writings are posted on the Army of God website, with the caption "Paul: American Hero" under his picture and the biblical passage, "Of whom the world was not worthy" (Hebrews 11:38). Hill's digital book, *Mix My Blood with the Blood of the Unborn*, is still available for downloading on the Army of God website.

Following the Hill shootings, abortion-clinic violence moved northward from Pensacola. In five of the next six years, during what became commonly known as the "killing season," abortion providers in northern New York State and Canada were attacked in the first week of November. All five victims were shot through a glass window or door at their homes, on or around Veterans' Day. It is possible that in this extremist "war," the "loyal soldiers" of the radical fringe groups appropriated the remembrance holiday for war veterans as a way to memorialize their own martyrs and those imprisoned for the cause. The extremist organizations even co-opted some of the symbols of real veterans' groups, for instance by using poppies on their anti-abortion posters.

James Kopp was added to the list of anti-abortion fanatics when he was finally captured and convicted in the killing of Dr. Barnett Slepian, the abortion provider in Buffalo, New York, who was fatally shot in his own kitchen as he was microwaving a bowl of soup while talking with his wife and one of his four children. Although the perpetrators in the other November shootings in Canada and northern New York State have not been identified, investigators speculate that Kopp is most likely responsible for all of them. In 2003, he was given the maximum sentence of twenty-five years to life in prison for the Slepian murder, and predictably he also became a martyr for the cause. Affectionately called the "Atomic Dog" on the extremist websites, Kopp continues to receive messages from fans through the Army of God e-mail system.[10]

Although the Canadian and New York State shootings ended abruptly with Kopp's arrest, the violence had already moved to Boston. On December 30, 1994, John Salvi stormed a pair of abortion clinics, killing two clinic workers and wounding five others. He was convicted of murder, but because Massachusetts does not have the death penalty, he was ordered to serve two consecutive life terms. In November 1996, however, Salvi was found dead in his maximum-security prison cell. Although his death was ruled a suicide by law-enforcement authorities, the Army of God has elevated Salvi to martyr status by claiming that he was murdered in prison.[11]

In a bizarre postscript to the Boston shootings, a clinic client, Deborah Gaines, filed lawsuits against Pre-Term Health Services and the owners of the Beacon Street building that housed the clinic. The suits asked for unspecified damages as well as lifetime costs associated with giving birth to her daughter, Vivian, and raising the child. Gaines had scheduled an appointment for an abortion at Pre-Term Health Services on the day of the shooting, and had just arrived at the clinic when she heard the gunshots. She recalled that she ran out of the clinic and never rescheduled the abortion; seven months later, she gave birth. Judge Patrick Brady allowed the lawsuit to go forward as Gaines's attorney claimed that his client was just trying to provide for her children: "She is not looking for megabucks for herself. She is looking to make the best life she can for her daughter." In her lawsuit, Gaines asserted that the shooting was a result of lax security at the clinic. But in an even stranger twist to the Salvi story, the two security guards who had been on duty that fateful day also sued the abortion facility and the building owners, saying that they were "emotionally traumatized" by the shootings.[12]

Legislators responded to the violence at abortion facilities by passing the "Freedom of Access to Clinic Entrances Act of 1994." This legislation set restrictions on the right to assemble near abortion clinics, and it had an immediate dampening effect on the number of blockades and the number of arrests at blockades surrounding abortion clinics. Although the shootings ended, the threats of violence by the anti-abortion fringe groups continued. The National Abortion Federation reports that in 2003 alone, there were 331 incidents of hate mail, harassing phone calls, and bomb threats made to abortion clinics. There have also been 554 anthrax hoaxes since clinics began recording such threats in 2002.[13]

Abortion-clinic bombings continued throughout the 1990s, attracting individuals who actually had less interest in ending abortion than in terrorism. Before he ever bombed his first abortion clinic, for instance, Eric Robert Rudolph began his terrorist activities by bombing the park adjacent to the 1996 Olympic Games in Atlanta. Using an elaborate pipe bomb loaded with nails and screws for extra destructive force, Rudolph hid the bomb in a knapsack, which was found by a security guard, Richard Jewell, before it detonated. Tragically, the device went off while security teams were trying to evacuate the Olympic Park area, killing one woman and injuring more than one hundred additional people. Lacking any substantial leads, the police initially focused on the security guard, Richard Jewell, as the suspect, while Rudolph escaped scrutiny entirely—and then began his abortion-clinic bombings. In January 1997, he used two bombs to injure several people in an attack at an abortion clinic in Atlanta. The following month, he bombed a gay nightclub in Atlanta, causing several injuries but no deaths, and in January 1998, he used two bombs to destroy an abortion-services facility in Birmingham, Alabama, where a police officer was killed and one nurse was critically injured. (The strategy of using tandem bomb attacks—the second targeting those who respond to the first—is a common terrorist tactic; it is one that the insurgents in Iraq are using.) Following the nightclub bombing and the Birmingham clinic attack, Rudolph sent letters to the authorities claiming responsibility for the attacks and promising more.

The Army of God lists Eric Rudolph as another of its "heroes." There are some who believe that members of the group may have helped him evade arrest over the next five years, much of which he spent as a fugitive in the Appalachian wilderness. During this time, he also became a cult hero for anti-government extremists. Two country-western songs were written about him, and there was a top-selling T-shirt that read: "Run, Rudolph, Run."[14]

Rudolph was finally arrested when he was caught rummaging through a dumpster for something to eat. Under a plea agreement in 2005 he was sentenced to four consecutive life terms without parole for the 1998 murder of the police officer who was killed when he responded to the Birmingham clinic bombing. Unrepentant for his violent actions, Rudolph continued to berate the government for assorted injustices at his sentencing.[15] His hatred of the government took priority over any concerns he may have had about abortion.

Eric Robert Rudolph has become a hero to white-supremacist organizations; in fact, there are close ties between the anti-abortion extremists and some radical skinhead and Aryan Nation subversive groups. United in their hatred of government policies that allow abortion and gay rights, these groups find hate-filled soul mates in their alliances. The Anti-Defamation League has issued warnings about the "extremist chatter" following the arrest of Eric Rudolph, describing it as a "dangerous mix of twisted conspiracy theories about Jews and calls to violence.... What some extremists are saying is, this person is a hero whose crusade against abortion and the government is noble and praiseworthy," according to Abraham Foxman, the ADL national director.[16]

FRINGE AND MAINSTREAM

Although the violence against abortion providers appears to have abated, the militancy of extremist organizations has had an impact on the mainstream, nonviolent pro-life organizations. Throughout the era of clinic shootings and bombings in the 1980s and 1990s, most legitimate anti-abortion organizations immediately disowned and distanced themselves from the actions of the violent fringe. But they were caught up in the back-draft from the violence and often found their right to free speech affected.

Indeed, in an attempt to deal with "potential violence" against abortion providers, law-enforcement personnel and the courts responded with alacrity to the demands for action from abortion providers like Planned Parenthood and abortion supporters like the National Organization for Women. In so doing, they have often failed to draw a distinction between fanatics in groups like the Army of God and leaders of nonviolent, mainstream pro-life organizations like the Pro-Life Action League. In fact, in what appears to be an attempt to bankrupt leaders of the anti-abortion movement, federal anti-racketeering laws known collectively as the Racketeer Influence and Corrupt Organizations Act of 1970 (RICO) have been used against some of the pro-life groups.

Originally enacted to bankrupt the Mafia and bring down organized-crime kingpins, RICO was used for the first time to bankrupt a nonprofit ideological organization in 1989, in a case against the Pro-Life Action League resulting from a federal lawsuit filed against them by the National Organization for Women. At the center of the RICO case was Joseph Scheidler, who founded the Pro-Life Action League in 1980. The mission of the Chicago-based anti-abortion organization was "to end abortion through non-violent direct action." From its founding, the key activities of the anti-abortion organization included maintaining "an abortion clinic presence" through prayer vigils outside the facilities and sidewalk counseling. On its website, the Pro-Life Action League suggests that "sidewalk counseling is the most important pro-life work God has given us to do. Praying outside abortion clinics is the first step in becoming directly involved in fighting abortion." In addition to its "abortion clinic presence," the Pro-Life Action League attempts to raise awareness of the injustice of abortion by way of marches, pickets, prayer vigils, and what it calls the "Face the Truth Tours," which involve exhibiting poster-size graphic photos of aborted fetuses in an effort to "show what abortion does to the unborn child." (While repugnant to most viewers—and purposefully so—the shocking photos of dismembered fetuses are still a form of speech that is protected under the First Amendment.) The Pro-Life Action League also attempts to confront the abortionists by picketing outside abortion facilities, at the front entrances of the offices of Planned Parenthood, and, in its most controversial activity, outside abortion providers' homes.

In addition to this direct action, the Pro-Life Action League provides educational services to other pro-life organizations by helping activists implement effective pro-life programs in their communities. The league provides training materials and conducts training workshops in many areas of nonviolent pro-life activism. A key resource is leader Joe Scheidler's book, *CLOSED: 99 Ways to Stop Abortion*. One of the ninety-nine tips offered is a severe warning against the use of violence. Written in 1985—long before the abortion-clinic shootings had even begun—Scheidler's book demands that "all of the activist pro-lifers affiliated with the Pro-Life Action League must concur with the League's position against violence and its program of non-violent direct action. We take our commitment to non-violence seriously, believing that violence on our part would be counter-productive. It is the abortionists who are engaged in routine violence against unborn children and their mothers. The use of violence could damage the reputation of pro-life activists while undermining traditional non-violent methods. The use of violence will reinforce the erroneous belief that the end justifies the means, and that evil can be overcome by evil."[17]

Despite this strong statement, the National Organization for Women identified the Pro-Life Action League as the real threat to its pro-choice activities. In an effort to silence the organization in 1986, NOW urged President Reagan, the U.S. Justice Department, Congress, and local law-enforcement agencies to respond to what began to be defined as the "subversive activities" of the Pro-Life Action League. When law enforcement was unable to find evidence that the organization was involved in criminal activities beyond trespassing, NOW assembled the Delaware Women's Health Organization and the Pensacola Ladies Center to file a lawsuit in federal district court. Based on a strategy developed by Eleanor Smeal, then the president of NOW, the lawsuit was brought under federal antitrust laws, and Scheidler was charged with a nationwide criminal conspiracy to close women's health clinics.[18] Thus began a twenty-year journey in the courts, culminating with three Supreme Court decisions and nearly a dozen lower-court battles. The goal for the women's groups was to put the Pro-Life Action League out of business and to bankrupt its leader, Joseph Scheidler, sending a chilling message to other pro-life advocacy organizations that they, too, would be ruined if they continued their direct-action tactics.

The National Organization for Women won the first battle in this war when the district court denied Scheidler's motion to dismiss the case. Emboldened, NOW then expanded the case against Scheidler and the Pro-Life Action League to include Randall Terry and Operation Rescue, a second nonviolent direct-action organization involved in the same kind of sidewalk counseling activities as the Pro-Life Action League. And, in an effort to strengthen the suit against the nonviolent anti-abortion organizations, NOW added charges of extortion and violation of federal racketeering laws in its lawsuit. The RICO Act was enlisted in this lawsuit because the financial penalties would be extremely stiff if the courts ruled against the group, allowing for triple damages.

In 1991, NOW suffered a setback when the lawsuit was dismissed by Judge James Holderman on the grounds that RICO required that the defendants have an economic motive for their activities. Since the Pro-Life Action League and Operation Rescue were nonprofit organizations that gained no financial benefit from their activities, the court ruled that they could not appropriately be prosecuted under the RICO Act. The Seventh Circuit Court of Appeals upheld the decision. But NOW, encouraged by public fears of violence at abortion clinics, brought the appeal to the U.S. Supreme Court. Arguing for the Pro-Life Action League, G. Robert Blakey, a professor at the University of Notre Dame law school and the architect of the RICO statutes, said that RICO indeed required an economic motive and was never designed to be used against public protest groups. Blakey's argument was lost on the Supreme Court, which ruled unanimously that RICO could indeed be used against such groups and sent the case back to district court.[19]

On September 22, 1995, district court judge David Coar granted NOW permission to take depositions from several people who were incarcerated for clinic shootings, even though these people had no ties with Scheidler and the Pro-Life Action League. NOW prepared subpoenas for inmates Paul Hill and Rachelle Shannon.[20] Their graphic testimony about the shooting of abortion providers was included in the case against Scheidler in order to show that the activities of the nonviolent organization contributed to a "pattern of violence"

Judge Coar continued to make rulings that strengthened NOW's lawsuit against the Pro-Life Action League. Then, in a historic move in 1997, Judge Coar designated *NOW v. Scheidler* a class-action lawsuit, certifying the feminist organization as the class representative of all women "whose rights to the services of women's health centers in the United States at which abortions are performed have been or will be interfered with by defendants' unlawful activities."[21] Coar also ruled that if NOW was determined to have proven its case, then the defendants would be held responsible for all the acts of terrorism and violence that other anti-abortion organizations orchestrated throughout the country.

Realizing that he could not possibly survive such a ruling, Randall Terry signed a settlement with NOW in December 1997, agreeing to the issuance of a twelve-year injunction against him. On January 7, 1998, Judge Coar granted preliminary approval of the settlement, which included steep fines if Terry violated the order by engaging in future clinic activities. With Randall Terry effectively out of the lawsuit—and out of the anti-abortion movement—opening arguments for the *NOW v. Scheidler* trial began in federal district court in Chicago in March 1998. Within a month, the jury had returned a unanimous verdict against Scheidler, finding that he had engaged in a nationwide conspiracy to deny women access to abortion clinics.[22] The jury also determined that he, Operation Rescue, the Pro-Life Action League, and their codefendants had engaged in twenty-one acts of extortion that qualified them as part of a criminal enterprise, and awarded two abortion clinics $85,926 in damages, which under the RICO Act would be tripled to a total of $257,780. Because the case was a class-action suit, more than nine hundred clinics across the country also had the opportunity to file for similar damages against Scheidler and the codefendants.

Scheidler kept on fighting, although the setbacks continued. On October 2, 2001, the Seventh Circuit Court of Appeals upheld the injunction against the Pro-Life Action League. The decision stated that the First Amendment does not protect "violent conduct" and that "violence in any form is the antithesis of reasoned discussion." The fact that the courts have never found any evidence that Scheidler's group had ever engaged in any form of violent activity seemed irrelevant. A defiant Scheidler mounted a new campaign called "Face the Truth," which brought dozens of pro-life volunteers carrying giant posters of aborted fetuses onto the sidewalks adjacent to high-traffic areas in major cities. With the Pro-Life Action League as an organization under siege by the pro-abortion movement, pro-life donations increased dramatically. Scheidler remarked, "The case never slowed us down. I would say it pepped us up. We didn't know how much time we had before we would be shut down permanently by the courts. We always knew, though, whether it's by us or someone else, the battle would go on because it is right."[23]

Scheidler's instincts were correct—there have indeed been subtle changes in the politics of abortion, reaching far beyond the pro-life advocacy community. Signs of these subtle shifts were evident in the response to the 2002 *NOW v. Scheidler* suit: even some pro-choice advocates were disturbed by the court ruling that RICO could be used in such a case. In an article entitled "RICO: Be Careful What You Wish For," Robyn Blumner acknowledged, "Yes, the executive director of the Pro-Life Action League, Joseph Scheidler, violated the law by trespassing on clinic property and dogging clinic workers. He used whatever non-violent tactics were at his disposal in trying to close down a concern that, to his mind, was in the business of infanticide." But, Blumner asked,

How different is that from the African Americans in the 1960s who defied segregationist, Jim Crow laws in the South by illegally parking themselves at whites-only lunch counters? Or, how different is the Pro-Life Action League's activities from that of Greenpeace activists who took it upon themselves to plug industrial pipes that were spewing toxic waste into the oceans? Or, General Motors workers in 1937 who staged a sit down strike occupying the plant so their union would be recognized? All were acts of conscience, of civil disobedience, and all were illegal. But, now, the civilly disobedient face not only jail, but financial ruin as well, and so do the organizations associated with them.[24]

The decision by NOW to file suit under RICO provisions began to boomerang on the organization, which was increasingly seen as pursuing an obsessive vendetta. (The legal analyst Jonathan Turley compared NOW to Captain Ahab and Joseph Scheidler to Moby Dick.)[25] And the Supreme Court agreed yet again to review *NOW v. Scheidler.* Oral arguments began on December 4, 2002, focusing on two important issues: (1) whether peacefully blocking the entrance to an abortion clinic or delaying a woman's access to a clinic constitutes the federal crime of "extortion," and (2) whether private parties like NOW and the abortion clinics can sue under RICO for the devastating penalty of a federal injunction against the "racketeers."

At this point, the political climate surrounding abortion rights and the use of the RICO act to prosecute anti-abortion advocacy organizations had heated up dramatically, with seventy-four individuals and organizations either filing or joining in others' amicus briefs. In a strange political twist, those filing briefs in support of Scheidler included, among others, People for the Ethical Treatment of Animals (PETA); the Maryknoll priest Rev. Roy Bourgeois, founder of School of the Americas Watch; and the death penalty activist Sister Helen Prejean, a Sister of St. Joseph and protagonist of *Dead Man Walking.* (Just one brief, from the Seamless Garment Network, included signatures from the Southern Christian Leadership Conference, the Voices in the Wilderness peace activists, and the Vieques Support Committee.) In his brief for PETA, Craig Bradley, a professor at the Indiana University School of Law, claimed that the case would have a negative effect on all advocacy groups but particularly on a group such as his client: "What the pro-life advocates did could not be considered extortion under the federal law because the law talks about obtaining property by threat. They wanted to shut the abortion clinics down. They did not want to take them over. Just like Scheidler's group, PETA protesters would only want to shut down an animal rendering plant, not take it over."[26]

The Thomas More Society Pro-Life Law Center chose the Washington, D.C., law firm of Robbins, Russell, Englert, Orseck & Untereiner to present the merits, briefs, and oral arguments for the Scheidler side. Solicitor General Ted Olson, representing the federal government, argued that the extortion charges could indeed apply to abortion-clinic blockades, but that the second injunction should be vacated. NOW attorney Fay Clayton attempted to defend both elements of the lower court's judgment. While the First Amendment right to free speech was not part of the case, early in the oral arguments Justice Anthony Kennedy interjected, "There is always a First Amendment implication in a protest case." Justice Antonin Scalia suggested that the broad definition of "obtaining property" in the lower-court judgment would constantly require the Court "to sort out whether that definition doesn't sail too close to the wind with respect to First Amendment rights."[27]

In his defense of Scheidler, Roy Englert argued that under the district court's ruling, the students who staged sit-ins to integrate southern lunch counters at Woolworth's in the 1960s could have been charged with extortion. Yet Fay Clayton defended the lower-court ruling by claiming that the language of the RICO statute does not restrict private parties like NOW from seeking injunctive relief. When Justice Stephen Breyer expressed concern that extortion charges could have been brought against protesters like those involved in the sit-ins of the civil-rights movement, Clayton retorted that "Martin Luther King didn't tell his followers to go into Woolworth's and bash people around." But Justice Scalia would not allow the casual (and unsubstantiated) suggestion of violence to go unchallenged this time.[28]

Realizing that things were not going well, NOW's president, Kim Gandy, held a press conference while the arguments were still being made before the Court to say that "NOW filed this suit only to protect women and clinic staff from a violent campaign to close abortion clinics nationwide. Since the nationwide injunction in *NOW v.*

Scheidler in July, 1999, there has been virtually no violence at abortion clinic protests. Protesters have continued their picketing, shouting, so-called sidewalk counseling and even abusive name calling—but without the violence. Stopping the violence was precisely our goal in this case."[29]

Nonetheless, on February 26, 2003, after seventeen years of litigation, the Supreme Court ruled 8-1 in Scheidler's favor, overturning the lower court. In his majority opinion, Chief Justice William Rehnquist wrote: "Because all of the predicate acts supporting the jury's finding of a RICO violation must be reversed, the judgment that petitions violated RICO must also be reversed. Without an underlying RICO violation, the District court's injunction must necessarily be vacated."[30]

With such decisive language, it would have appeared that *NOW v. Scheidler* would finally end. But NOW attorney Fay Clayton, unwilling to concede defeat, convinced the appellate court that there was a possibility that the Supreme Court had overlooked four "predicate acts" that might allow the injunction to remain in force. On June 28, 2005, Joe Scheidler and the Pro-Life Action League learned that they would be making yet another trip to the Supreme Court. As the final act of their 2004 term, the Court granted certiorari to the Pro-Life Action League's petition of an appellate-court ruling that would have prolonged the landmark RICO case, now reaching its twentieth year. As Scheidler prepared for his third appearance before the U.S. Supreme Court in 2006, a lien remained on his home and more than $400,000 in an escrow account for NOW. The week after he received notice about the upcoming Court battle, he participated in Pro-Life Action League's sixth annual "Face the Truth Tour" in July 2005. The nine-day event found Scheidler and his band of volunteers visiting sites throughout Chicago and other Illinois cities, displaying their enormous anti-abortion signs to passersby. They added pictures of newborn babies to the dozens of pictures of aborted fetuses in an effort to remind viewers that "these are real babies we are talking about."[31]

Finally, on February 28, 2006, the Supreme Court ruled 8-0 that abortion clinics cannot rely on federal laws against racketeering and extortion to prevent demonstrations against abortion.[32] The opinion, written by Stephen Breyer, stated that clinics could not use the decades-old Hobbs Act, which outlaws the obstruction of commerce by "robbery or extortion," to stymie protesters. Justice Breyer wrote that "Physical violence unrelated to robbery or extortion falls outside the Hobbs Act's scope," and that trying to use the act as the National Organization for Women has done "broadens the Hobbs Act's scope well beyond what case law has assumed."[33] Moreover, the ruling noted, "Congress specifically addressed the needs of abortion clinics and their patients in 1994, when it passed legislation that makes it a federal crime to attack or blockade abortion clinics, their operators or their patrons. By its actions in 1994, Congress suggested that the much older Hobbs Act did not address anti-abortion protests."[34]

While the Pro-Life Action League celebrated the Supreme Court decision as a victory for the First Amendment, the president of NOW, Kim Gandy, published an angry statement on the organization's website decrying the Court's actions: "By vacating the injunction on narrow, technical grounds, the Supreme Court sided today with thugs and bullies, not peaceful protesters." Gandy warned that the ruling would "add to the increasing difficulty women face in obtaining reproductive health services," and she promised that "if the Court's 8-0 decision in Scheidler, et al v National Organization for Women ushers in a return to clinic violence in the United States, NOW stands ready to fight in every jurisdiction."[35] To prepare for such attacks on abortion-service delivery, Gandy promised additional legal action and vowed to make available a legal kit that local clinics and lawyers can use to enforce the 1994 Freedom of Access to Clinic Entrances Act in their communities: "We must do whatever is necessary to protect doctors and patients, or our legal right to abortion will be a hollow shell."[36] In her press release, Gandy called Joseph Scheidler "a leader of the pro-life mafia who has vowed to stop abortion by any means necessary, and the ensuing attacks included arson, bombings, violent blockades, death threats and even murder."[37]

Now that the Supreme Court has ruled in such a decisive way, Scheidler is hoping that the judgment against him will be reversed and the bond that still includes his Chicago home will be released. Scheidler has promised a "resurgence of pro-life activism" as the publicity surrounding his victory in his third appearance before the

CHAPTER FIVE

The Politics
of Celebration

WHILE SOME ON the pro-choice side regard abortion as a sad necessity, many others view the successful provision of abortion services to women as a cause for celebration. In fact, for the last several years there has been an annual event honoring the "heroism" of abortion providers.

Promotional materials for the National Day of Appreciation for Abortion Providers exhort: "On this day…Stand up with your abortion services providers and say: Thank you for your heroism, perseverance, courage and commitment to women." Much like Valentine's Day, participants are expected to give gifts of love and appreciation to those who "make abortion safe and legal." Gift suggestions include flowers, candy, or a "breakfast basket of fruit or muffins." Likening this occasion to a holy day, there is a "sermon and prayer" for abortion providers on the part of the Religious Coalition for Reproductive Choice.[1] Calling abortion a "sacred choice," some within the religious community, like dissident Catholic theologian and Marquette University professor Daniel C. Maguire, have used the National Day of Appreciation for Abortion Providers to help transform what was once viewed as a shameful act into a God-given right.[2]

The abortion appreciation holiday was first celebrated on

October 26, 1996, by Refuse and Resist, an organization whose website also demands that we "Free Mumia Abu-Jamal" and "End the Unjust Occupation of Iraq." Refuse and Resist initiated the day as part of the "October Month of Resistance," declaring on their website: "This is a day, so urgently needed.... It concentrates on the struggle for women's reproductive rights—bridging the gap between providers and activists, helping to unify providers and rallying people from all walks of life to stand in solidarity with those who are literally putting their lives on the line every day so that women have the right to choose."

Refuse and Resist is a fringe group; the real money behind the National Day of Appreciation for Abortion Providers comes from sources that are decidedly mainstream: the Ford, Hewlett, Packard, Buffett, and Turner foundations.[3] Moreover, the holiday is endorsed by such mainstream pro-choice groups as the American Civil Liberties Union and the National Abortion Rights Action League, as well as Planned Parenthood, the National Organization for Women, Medical Students for Choice, Catholics for a Free Choice, the Boston Women's Health Book Collective, *Ms. Magazine,* and others.[4]

On its inaugural, the Appreciation Day was launched with a press conference and rally in Washington, D.C. Receptions honoring abortion providers were held in cities all over the United States. In most locales, the occasion was uneventful—except in Chicago, where pro-life leader Joseph Scheidler and a large number of other pro-life protesters set up a picket line outside the appreciation reception site, Chicago's Heartland Café. Angry outbursts ensued and one member of the pro-choice contingent destroyed a six-by-eight-foot pro-life sign. The Chicago police arrived and arrested a member of Refuse and Resist on charges of criminal destruction of property.

Organizers of the pro-abortion holiday created a kit filled with useful documents and forms that volunteers can use as aids for arranging celebrations in their own hometowns. The kit includes artistic posters, sample press releases, and a video, *The Life of Dr. David Gunn,* about the slain abortion provider. There is also a pro-choice poem by the prizewinning playwright Reg E. Gaines, written for presentation to abortion providers, and a letter of thanks written by Medical Students for Choice.[5] Bringing angry activism into the celebration, Refuse and Resist urges volunteers to "Organize demonstrations against the attack on women's rights. Politicians, clerics, and other bozos who call for patriarchal control over women deserve to be interrupted, shouted down, and run off." Refuse and Resist provides volunteers with written materials that compare "anti-choice zealots" with Adolf Hitler and assert that "outlawing abortion was and is a Nazi Program." Volunteers are advised that "today's anti-abortionists, who bomb women's clinics, murder doctors, harass women seeking abortions, preach a male dominated family, and espouse the subordination of women to the state and church as 'breeders,' can certainly identify with a record like Hitler's."

Like other advocacy groups, Refuse and Resist sees a paternalistic "plot" behind the pro-life agenda. "There is more at stake here than a group of religious fanatics trying to impose their views on everyone else," the organization darkly warns. "The issue of abortion is the doorway through which many people are brought to the broader reactionary agenda of restoring America's 'glory' as the undisputed imperial power in the world and upholding conservative domination at home. Maintaining the 'sanctity of motherhood' which keeps women at home and subservient to the father and the state, is part and parcel of this. Right to Life means Father Right and Fatherland uber alles!" For the Refuse and Resist organizers, the right-to-life movement is nothing more than central headquarters for the "proto-fascist popular action forces." Their foundational statement proclaims: "To the Reaganites, racists, misogynists, televangelists, would be Rambos, war planners, and America-firsters, we say the future is not yours!"[6]

A day of angry celebration for abortion may not be for everyone, so the pro-choice community offers other ways to celebrate abortion in a more personal way. Planned Parenthood's website store offers hats, T-shirts and lollipops shaped like packaged condoms to celebrate choice. Each of the past four years, Planned Parenthood has offered its distinctive Christmas cards, which proudly proclaim "Choice on Earth," although the organization caused some controversy when it unveiled T-shirts bearing the slogan "I had an abortion."[7]

"I'M NOT SORRY DAY"

Publicly appreciating abortion providers is just one way in which the pro-choice community has escalated its attempts to convince the public that abortion is not only the right choice, but also one that can and should be embraced with joy and enthusiasm. Despite a growing body of evidence pointing to post-abortion trauma for women, the fathers of their babies, and sometimes their extended families and friends, the pro-choicers are committed to convincing others that abortion is not merely a melancholy necessity but an act that makes women's lives better. In fact, instead of joining the march on Washington every January 22 to commemorate the anniversary of *Roe v. Wade,* many in the pro-choice community will celebrate "I'm Not Sorry Day," sharing personal stories about the ways in which their abortions improved their lives.

The I'm Not Sorry movement was created in 2003 by Patricia Beninato of Richmond, Virginia. According to an article in *The Nation,* Beninato "became annoyed" on the thirtieth anniversary of *Roe v. Wade* because "every time she turned on the news, anti-choicers were yelling about babies being slaughtered or erroneously claiming that women who have abortions are destined for clinical depression."[8] The thirty-seven-year-old customer-service representative thought, "I had an abortion, and I'm glad I did. Someone should put up a website for women who had abortions and don't regret it." Since Beninato was then "between jobs," she decided she would be that someone. Thus, www.imnotsorry.net was founded and has since gathered more than one hundred stories.

Jennifer Baumgardner (designer of the "I Had an Abortion" T-shirts) was so moved by Beninato's I'm Not Sorry initiative that she launched a campaign to recast the *Roe* anniversary, January 22, as I'm Not Sorry Day. This project consisted of three elements: a film directed by Gillian Aldrich documenting women's experiences with abortion, the I Had an Abortion T-shirts, and a postcard that lists resources such as post-abortion counseling and the National Network of Abortion Funds. The message of the day is that "women made the right decision."[9]

Katha Pollitt applauded the I'm Not Sorry movement in her "Subject to Debate" column in *The Nation:* "As an antidote to the antichoice propaganda that presents abortion as an inevitable source of shame, sorrow and regret—and pro-choice pablum about what a painful choice it is—take a look at the I'm Not Sorry website where women are posting positive stories about abortions that left them flooded with relief, eager to move on, and more self-reliant.... The site revives the old feminist idea of Abortion without Apology—and not a moment too soon."[10]

Like the I'm Not Sorry group, the Feminist Women's Health Center website invites women to share the reasons they made their "choice." One woman, Emily, wrote of her aborted child that "I loved her enough to send her back to God." Another, Nicky, was slightly more ambivalent: "The decision made me sad but never once have I regretted it." There are plans to produce what the Feminist Women's Health Center describes as a "zine" by the name of "Our Truths/Nuestras Verdades," which "aims to break the silence that many women face, providing a forum for women to share their stories about abortion, and to affirm their decisions and experiences." As the editors say, "submissions from women who have had abortions receive priority; however, friends and support people of women who have had abortions are welcome to submit work as well."

HOLLYWOOD CELEBRATES ABORTION

Feminist advocacy groups have been able to look to Hollywood for support in disseminating the "celebrate abortion" message. In 2004, Imelda Staunton's portrayal of Vera Drake, a "courageous" abortionist, won Best Actress nominations for nearly every motion-picture award given, including the Oscar. Despite the lack of popular appeal and dismal box-office receipts, the film *Vera Drake* won the Best Film award at the Venice International Film Festival, and director Mike Leigh won the Gotham Lifetime Achievement Award. Vera Drake was one of Hollywood's favorite heroines—the kindly abortionist with a heart of gold. Critic Roger Ebert's review describes Staunton's Drake as a "melodious plum pudding of a woman who is always humming or singing to herself." Ebert claims that "the movie is not about abortion so much as about families. The Drakes are close and loving. Vera's husband, who works with his brother in an auto repair shop, considers his wife a treasure." Hollywood loves movies about kindly abortion providers and rewards them whenever possible. The 1999 Oscar for Best Actor went to Michael Caine for his role as the friendly abortionist in *The Cider House Rules.*

In the 1980s and 1990s, an increasing number of movies portrayed abortion in a positive light. The coveted President's Award went to the pro-abortion HBO movie *If These Walls Could Talk* at the Emmy Awards ceremony in 1997. The made-for-television movie was not nominated in any other meaningful category for acting or screenplay; the only other Emmy nominations it received were one for "outstanding editing" and one for "outstanding hairstyling for a miniseries." It won neither award. In the hairstyling category, *If These Walls Could Talk* lost out to the presumably better-coifed *Mrs. Santa Claus.*

Celebrating abortion before and after *Roe,* the film takes the viewer to a single house in an unnamed midsized American city during three different time periods. The first segment takes place in 1952, when we meet Claire Donnelly, a nurse played by Demi Moore whose husband has been killed in the Korean War. A short affair with her brother-in-law leaves her with an unwanted pregnancy. Abortion is illegal at the time, so viewers get a graphic glimpse of the horrors of the notorious back-alley coat-hanger abortion. In the second segment, set in 1974, when abortion had recently been legalized, Sissy Spacek plays the married mother of four whose unexpected pregnancy has challenged the family's finances. Her husband must reconsider his early retirement and their daughter may have trouble paying for college because of this new burden on the family. Worse, the heroine now may have to give up her desire to return to school and finish her own education. The Spacek character chooses to have the child, but the decision is a good one because abortion is then a legal option. The third segment, set in 1996 and directed by Cher, focuses upon Christine Cullen, played by Anne Heche, who becomes pregnant through an affair with her architecture professor just as the local abortion clinic has become the target of fanatical anti-abortion activists. As in most Hollywood portrayals of the courageous abortionist, Cher (who acts as well as directs) is eventually destroyed by the pro-life movement.

Indeed, from the earliest days of the pro-choice movement, the media have supported the idea that abortion is the good and noble choice—and that all opposition to it is evil. *A Private Matter,* a 1992 film starring serial pro-choice star Sissy Spacek, provides a "real life" example of a pre-*Roe* dilemma. Spacek plays Sherri Finkbine, the host of *Romper Room,* an Arizona children's television program. In 1962, Finkbine had taken the tranquilizer thalidomide during her pregnancy. After learning that thalidomide caused serious birth defects, Finkbine managed to obtain an abortion, although the law in Arizona at the time allowed abortion only when childbirth posed a risk to the mother's life. Hoping to warn others about the drug, the heroine tells her story to a newspaper reporter, who promises her anonymity. But when her name is disclosed to the world by the evil pro-lifers during legal proceedings, the legality of her abortion is questioned, and Finkbine and her family are under siege. Viewers learn that Finkbine feels powerless in the face of pressure exerted by her husband and the male judges involved in the case. A heroic yet tragic figure who is truly alone in her plight until she finally garners the strength to fight back, Spacek's Finkbine ends the movie engaged in a screaming match with her husband in her back yard as she calls him a coward for not supporting her abortion. The message is clear: women cannot rely on men to assist them in the good fight.

Like activist groups and show biz, liberal lawmakers too applaud abortion. In January 2004, California's Democrat-controlled state assembly passed a controversial resolution urging Americans to "celebrate" abortion and the *Roe v. Wade* decision.[11] Passed on the thirty-first anniversary of the Supreme Court ruling and supported by every Democratic member in the assembly, the resolution called on Congress and President Bush to "uphold the intent and substance of the 1973 United States Supreme Court decision" and urged Americans to "participate in the national celebration, 'The March for Women's Lives,' on April 25, 2004."

Many members of the nontraditional clergy have also joined the celebration. For more than twenty years, the Unitarian Universalist Association of Brooklyn has had its own "celebration" (they use the word in their "abortion services") of the anniversary of *Roe v. Wade* each January. The journalist Rod Dreher recalls his visit to the church on one of these occasions: "Sunday morning, Pastor Frederick Wooden, just back from the antiwar march in Washington, DC, stood at the door of the beautiful 19th century church warmly greeting parishioners coming in from the cold.... Then the adult congregation heard the first of three readings. The first was offered by an elderly woman named Marge, who read from the work of a feminist philosopher, who proclaimed abortion an integral part of women's liberation, the latest stage in women's revolt against marital dependence and female subjugation."[12] A young woman then gave a reading from the Holy Writ, taken from the Supreme Court's majority decision in *Roe*. Dreher writes that a black Baptist clergyman by the name of Carlton W. Veazey, head of the national Religious Coalition for Reproductive Choice, served as a guest preacher. In his sermon, Veazey told the congregation that when he began his full-time ministry on behalf of legal abortion five years ago, some were surprised to see a black man taking a leadership role in the fight: "I informed them that the black community has invested more in this effort because we know what it means to be without choice in so many areas."[13]

Celebrating abortion as a "God-given right," to use Veazey's phrase, is not restricted to the stereotypically liberal and ideologically marginal Unitarian Universalist Association. Currently, the Episcopal Church, the Presbyterian Church, the United Church of Christ, the United Methodist Church, the Unitarian Universalist Association, and Reform Judaism all have official statements in support of reproductive choice as a matter of conscience, adopted by their governing bodies.[14] While most of these statements cannot be viewed as explicitly "celebrating" abortion, all support the right to choose abortion as they once supported the more orthodox religious injunction to "choose life." As the following chapter will point out, in fact, some religious leaders view abortion not just as a choice, but as a "sacred choice."

CHAPTER SIX

Sacred Choices

M**ANY IN THE** pro-choice community draw upon the teachings of pro-choice clergy and theologians to assert that abortion is a "sacred and holy choice." They are supported in this view by several churches and other religious organizations, as well as by theologians like Daniel Maguire, who in his book *Sacred Choices* asserts that the major religions—including Islam and the Roman Catholic Church—all support an absolute, God-given right to abortion and that for women who undergo this procedure, "All of their choices, including their choice for abortion, are holy and healthy."[1] In the 2004 March for Women's Lives in Washington, D.C., the Religious Coalition for Reproductive Choice (RCRC) played a central role, providing the convocation and opening prayer. In a speech symbolically delivered at the Reflecting Pool in the nation's capital, the Reverend Katherine Hancock Ragsdale, an Episcopal priest and RCRC board member, sought to channel Dr. Martin Luther King Jr.'s 1963 speech at the same locale:[2]

> I have a dream of a world where every person has full access to all the health care they require provided conveniently and compassionately.
>
> I dream of a world where people don't grasp at the ridiculous and faithless notion that there is or can be a rule for every occasion and

that knowing and enforcing enough rules will save us from the difficult work of making complex ethical decisions.

I dream of a world that values cooperation over competition, compassion over punishment, respect over control, and the dazzling diversity of creation over conformity. I dream of a world that not only protects a woman's right to choose—but celebrates it.

The president and CEO of the RCRC, the Reverend Carlton W. Veazey, an African American, is ordained in the National Baptist Convention—as was Dr. King. And, like King, Rev. Veazey describes himself as "under attack" from those who wish to curb our freedom. In his "Letter from the President" in the fall/winter 2004 RCRC newsletter, *Faith and Choice,* Veazey wrote, "The Religious Right has used everything in its arsenal to turn faith into a political weapon against reproductive rights, but thanks to your personal commitment, the religious pro-choice community is countering the assault."[3]

In an effort to mobilize the crowd at the March for Women's Lives, Veazey also tried to echo King in praising the sacred right to abortion: "The time has come for the religious people of this country to proclaim with all our moral power that women's rights are also civil rights and human rights." The theme of the RCRC brochure, "Clergy for Choice Network," is Micah 6:8, which asks: "What does the Lord require of you but to do justice…?" Veazey spoke for many in the RCRC when he said that the coalition "has a special call" to support abortion.[4]

The Religious Coalition for Reproductive Choice is composed of forty national organizations from Christian and Jewish denominations, movements, and faith-based groups, as well as Unitarian, humanist, and ethical associations. These member bodies and many individuals subscribe to the RCRC's stated mission:[5]

> The Religious Coalition for Reproductive Choice brings the moral power of religious communities to ensure reproductive choice through education and advocacy. The Coalition seeks to give clear voice to the reproductive issues of people of color, those living in poverty, and other underserved populations.

In an attempt to recruit additional clergy to the pro-choice cause, the RCRC recently launched what it calls a "groundbreaking seminary course (that any Protestant seminaries can choose to adopt by simply requesting the curriculum from the RCRC) entitled, 'Theology and Reproductive Choice.'"[6] Designed by Dr. Laurel Schneider, associate professor of theology, ethics, and culture at the Chicago Theological Seminary, and reviewed by a panel of three theologians, the course is intended to "develop and prepare the next generation of pro-choice clergy." It will provide opportunities to further the pro-choice agenda that already exists in many seminaries today.

Currently there are active Seminarians for Choice groups at United Theological Seminary in Minneapolis, Eden Theological Seminary in St. Louis, Harvard Divinity School, Princeton Theological Seminary, the Graduate Theological Union in Berkeley, Union Theological Seminary in New York, and Boston University School of Theology. These groups sponsor campus worship services to celebrate the *Roe v. Wade* anniversary, hold "Peaceful Presence" events in support of local abortion clinics, and host and participate in "All Options Clergy Counseling" workshops for seminary students. The student leadership of Seminarians for Choice meets annually in Washington, D.C., to share ideas and learn about reproductive-choice issues in a national context.[7]

The RCRC provides teachers and students at the institution as well as clergy and congregations generally with prayers, sermons, and commentaries from Jewish and Christian perspectives, to use in special pro-choice religious services. Rabbi Bonnie Margulis, an RCRC staff member, offered the Jewish viewpoint on the anniversary:

> Rabbinic commentators from the Middle Ages to modern times agree that therapeutic abortion is not only warranted, it is actually mandated in Jewish law when a woman's life is at stake. For while the fetus is considered potential life—precious and sacred—it is not of equal status with the actual life of the woman, and therefore fetal life cannot take precedence over the life of the woman. As the 19th Century scholar Rabbi Moses Sofer wrote, "No woman is required to build up the world by destroying herself." As Jews, we celebrate the anniversary of Roe v. Wade because it has saved women's lives. And in Judaism there is no higher value than *pikuach, nefesh*, saving a life.

Margulis concluded her commentary with praise for the "holy work of abortion":

Because we are talking about much more than abortion, because we are talking about the social and economic injustices in our society that both make abortion necessary and so often make it inaccessible to those who need it, I believe we are commanded by God, the prophets and our own moral consciences to stand up and speak out to ensure justice and freedom of choice for all. And this is truly holy work. *Ken yehi ratzon*—let it be God's will.[8]

Likewise, the Reverend Robert Tiller, a Protestant minister associated with the RCRC, maintains that abortion is "holy." In his celebration of the anniversary of *Roe v. Wade,* Tiller draws from scripture to show that "Jesus' teachings emphasized the religious freedom and moral agency of each person, male or female." Like Margulis, Tiller makes a distinction between "potential life" and "actual life":

Some Christians believe that life begins at conception and therefore abortion is wrong. They are entitled to that perspective, even though both the biblical basis and the historical basis for it are flimsy. However, we must also acknowledge that millions of Christians—indeed a majority of Protestants in this country—have a different view believing instead that a fertilized egg is potential life, but not actual life. These Christians hold that the life, health, freedom, and moral agency of the pregnant woman are more important than the potential life in her womb.[9]

In a critical study of the RCRC, Michael Gorman, a theology professor at St. Mary's Seminary and University in Baltimore, and Ann Loar Brooks, an Episcopalian laywoman, write that "the RCRC sees itself not merely as a coalition of religious organizations and individuals, but as an organization with a divine calling and mission." An opening litany for "interfaith, pro-choice worship" begins with the leader proclaiming, "Rejoice, for you are called to freedom. You are called to worship and to adore your God, each in your own way and of your own time." The RCRC's book of prayers, entitled *Prayerfully Pro-Choice,* advises readers to "Pray for freedom to choose—to choose to have children, but also to choose not to have children.... Give us strengthened dedication as we seek reproductive freedom.... Let us never be satisfied until each person and each group is extended reproductive freedom."[10]

Throughout its literature, the RCRC maintains that the deci-

sion for abortion is a "holy act." In a "Service of Memory and Dedication" there is a prayer for "all those persons both lay and clergy
who do your holy work of listening to and helping women sort out
their options." "Affirming a Choice," by the feminist theologian
Diann Neu, is prefaced by an assertion that women's friends, minis-
ters, and counselors "need to develop and celebrate liturgies that
affirm women's reproductive choices, thus this liturgy affirms that a
woman has made a good and holy decision to have an abortion."[11]

The RCRC blesses those who provide abortion services: "Also
holy is the work of those who assist women in exercising their free
choice." In a 1997 sermon to the National Abortion Federation
(including doctors, administrators, and counselors in abortion provision), Katherine Hancock Ragsdale compared the "difficult" and
"dangerous" work of abortion providers to that of civil-rights leaders. Then, she likened the plight of abortionists to that of the
persecuted prophets whom Jesus mentions in the Beatitudes
(Matthew 5:11–12): "Blessed are you when people revile you and
persecute you falsely on my account, for in the same way they persecuted the prophets who were before you." In conclusion, Ragsdale
called upon a feminine deity: "May She bless us all and grant each
of us a full measure of faith and courage as we commit ourselves to
this sacred work."[12]

Knowing how compelling a religious message can be, the
RCRC advises its affiliates to develop religious convocations at the
local level to "bear faithful witness for choice." It recommends that
instead of a press conference to announce such a convocation, an
"alternative visibility event might be to gather members of the
clergy and political leaders appearing in front of a clinic that provides abortion services to bless the work they do as a powerful
symbol of support for reproductive choice."[13] Thus the Reverend
Cynthia Blumb, a United Church of Christ minister and executive
director of the Missouri RCRC, offered a blessing at a new Planned
Parenthood facility for the "holy work and service provided by
God's people on behalf of God's people." She also prayed for
"God's gracious blessing upon this work, upon this facility, and
upon all those who will pass through these doors." The blessing
concluded, "May Planned Parenthood continue to be an instru-
ment of your service, doing the holy work of healing and caring for

your creation, O Holy One, may it be so. And let the people say, Amen."

In a "Ceremony for Closure after an Abortion," the Reverend Kendyl Gibbons of the Unitarian Universalist Church affirms choice without qualification and suggests that guilt or feelings of loss can be transcended:

> We have gathered today to honor the importance of a decision.... We give them our support in the act by which they would release the energy and creativity which might have been their child, from the bonds of their grief and guilt, into the fathomless universe of potential, there to find other form.... With loving grief, we release that potential to other incarnations in the infinite womb of the universe, from which nothing is ever lost.[14]

While Gibbons' New Age perspective on the "infinite womb" of the universe is unusual, many mainstream theologians and religious leaders contend that the Christian, Jewish, and even Islamic traditions all allow for abortion. The book *Sacred Choices: The Right to Contraception and Abortion in Ten World Religions,* for instance, "shows that the right to an abortion is solidly grounded in the world's great religions," as Marquette University theologian Daniel C. Maguire writes in the preface. He adds the comment, "Sometimes the ending of incipient life is the best that life offers. Historically, women have been the principal cherishers and caretakers of life. We can trust them with these decisions."[15] Maguire argues that the ten religions presented in his book "defend what should be the obvious human right to contraception, and the moral and human right to an abortion when necessary."[16] To defend his assertion that even Islam and the Roman Catholic Church acknowledge the right to "end incipient life," he enlists the aid of theologians, many of them with academic appointments. Each chapter introduces the "authority figure" or "spiritual guide" who then reveals what the specific religion under discussion really says about abortion.

In an opening chapter, "The Roman Catholic Freeing of Conscience," Maguire dismisses the pope's authority in the matter of abortion with the remark: "States that do not have any population problem—in one particular case, even no births at all (Vatican City)—are doing their best, their utmost, to prevent the world from making sensible decisions regarding family planning."[17] He then turns to his "expert" theologian or "guide," Christine Gudorf, a professor at the International University in Miami, who says that "Christianity was born in a world in which contraception and abortion were both known and practiced. The Egyptians, Jews, Greeks and Romans used a variety of contraception methods.... Abortion appears to have been a widespread phenomenon." Gudorf maintains that Catholic teaching on contraception and abortion has been "anything but consistent." What most people think of as the "Catholic position on abortion," she claims, is actually quite recent and dates only from the 1930 encyclical *Casti Connubii* of Pope Pius XI. Prior to that, Gudorf says, Catholic Church teaching on abortion was a "mixed bag."[18]

Relying on Professor Gudorf's "authority," Maguire asserts that "neither the pro-choice nor the anti-choice tradition of the Catholic Church is more Catholic than the other." And, he adds, "By unearthing this authentic openness in the core of the tradition to choice on abortion and contraception, the status of the anti-choice position is revealed as only one among many Catholic views."[19] Drawing on the writings of St. Thomas Aquinas, the greatest of all Catholic thinkers, Maguire presents the theory of delayed animation or "ensoulment" as proof that even the "most esteemed of medieval theologians" allowed abortion.

While Maguire attempts to make a case that abortion is part of the Catholic tradition, he goes even further at the end of the chapter when he claims that the Church not only allows abortion, but celebrates it by rewarding some pro-choice individuals with sainthood. "Many Catholics," he writes, "do not know that there exists a pro-choice Catholic saint who was also an archbishop and a Dominican."[20] This was St. Antoninus, a fifteenth-century archbishop of Florence.

A quick Internet search indicates that Maguire's pronouncements on the "patron saint of abortion" are part of an urban legend in the pro-choice community. Not only did St. Antoninus never support abortion, he was one of the earliest in the Church to condemn it as an "abomination." Indeed, Antoninus has long been adopted by the pro-life community as their own patron saint. The St. Antoninus Institute for Catholic Education in Business notes that its pro-life inspiration comes from its namesake and holds that "the murdering of innocent lives, which abortion constitutes, is an absolute evil. Should corporations elect to engage themselves in a pursuit of ethical conduct they should do their utmost to combat this most dreadful moral plague of abortion which weakens our modern society, let alone cease to contribute themselves to this moral abomination."[21]

Maguire steadfastly argues that not only Catholicism but also Islam has historically been pro-choice. Despite strong prohibitions against abortion in official Islamic teaching, Maguire's "guide" to Islamic views on abortion, Riffat Hassan, a professor at the University of Louisville and a native of Pakistan, maintains that the "no-choice view is not the prevailing view in Islam.... There is broad acceptance in the major Islamic schools of law on the permissibility of abortion in the first four months of pregnancy."[22]

From Hassan's perspective, the principle called *ijithad* is central to Muslim ethics, and, indeed, to any true religious ethic. *Ijithad* means analyzing the unique data of a moral problem and arguing from Qur'anic principles, using analogy and logic to come to the best and most reasonable solution. This allows "Islamic ethics" to respond realistically to new problems for which there is no prescribed answer in the Qur'an. On this basis, Hassan claims that Islam justifies contraception and abortion for "reasons of health, economics, preservation of the woman's appearance, and improving the quality of offspring. This last reason is important in Islam because the Islamic approach to contraception has a social conscience. It is concerned with the common good. Producing sickly, weak or underdeveloped or uneducated children is not good for the *umma,* the society."[23]

In the chapter on "Judaism and Family Planning," Maguire enlists Laurie Zoloth, professor of Jewish studies at San Francisco State University, as his principal guide to discuss Judaism's support for abortion. Zoloth says, "In Judaism, there is room for vigorous debate with contradictory opinions heard and honored.... In Judaism it is the totality of life the Jewish belief is after—the inescapable call of the stranger, the constancy of the demand for justice in every interaction, and the importance of the minute details of daily life."[24] For Zoloth, the book of Exodus does not give the fetus equal standing with a born person: "Fetal tissue is human but not yet person." She tells us that in Judaism, "abortion is permitted as a health procedure since a fetus is not seen as being an ensouled person. Not only are the first forty days of conception considered like water, but also even in the last trimester, the fetus has a lesser moral status. The fetus is not deemed a *nefesh*, a person, until the head emerges in the birthing process."[25] Maguire concludes that for Jews, abortion is a *mitzvah*—a sacred duty.

Throughout *Sacred Choices,* Daniel Maguire maintains that the right to choose an abortion has deep religious roots. Thus he regards any laws that deny women this right as unjust and a violation of religious freedoms. "Such restrictive laws unduly privilege religious persons who espouse the most conservative views while disenfranchising those who hold equally religious grounded pro-choice views."[26] While certainly in the minority among Catholics, Maguire is not the only Catholic theologian to hold these views. As the following chapter will show, there are many professors of theology and religious studies on college campuses throughout the country attempting to convince a susceptible student body that abortion is often the "sacred choice" for women.

CHAPTER SEVEN

Catholics and the Politics of Abortion

O F ALL THE contested terrain in the abortion wars, the question of Catholic teaching on the subject has attracted the most attention and generated the most contentious debate. Rightly or wrongly, pro-choice activists and politicians have identified the Church as the final citadel standing against abortion, which means that its influence must be diminished or its commitment shown to be of questionable provenance. But notwithstanding all the criticism by organizations like Catholics for a Free Choice and the assertions by writers like Daniel Maguire about a golden age of abortion, official Catholic teaching on abortion as published in the Catechism of the Catholic Church is very clear: "Human life must be respected and protected absolutely from the moment of conception."

From the earliest days of the Church, abortion has been viewed as a serious offense. Indeed, the Catechism clearly states that "since the first century, the Church has affirmed the moral evil of every procured abortion." It also maintains that the Church has been consistent on the matter of abortion: "This teaching has not changed and remains unchangeable.... Direct abortion, that is to say, abortion willed either as an end or a means, is gravely contrary to the moral law.... Life must be protected with the utmost care from the moment of conception: abortion and infanticide are abominable crimes."[1] Church teaching has been unambiguous: "From the first moment of his existence, a human being must be recognized as having the rights of a person—among which is the inviolable right of every innocent being to life." Despite the clarity of these pronouncements, some Catholic theologians, philosophers, and advocacy organizations have committed themselves to debunking the catechetical teachings.

For example, in their *Brief, Liberal, Catholic Defense of Abortion,* Daniel Dombrowski and Robert Deltete, both professors of philosophy at the Jesuit-led Seattle University, assert that the reasons why the Church forbade abortion were based on erroneous assumptions about conception and life. Dombrowski and Deltete claim that St. Augustine viewed abortion as evil only because it destroyed the purpose of marriage and marital sexual relations—specifically, procreation. In addition, they claim that Augustine's early writings referred to the life growing in the womb as merely a "seed" that needed to develop and flourish. They conclude that Augustine regarded the fetus at the earliest stages as simply "plant life."

Likewise, the authors argue that because there is no article on abortion in the *Summa theologica,* therefore St. Thomas Aquinas, the Church's most important intellectual force, was "not really interested" in the subject. But while his ontological argument on abortion was rudimentary, Aquinas did believe that there was life in the womb from conception. Although he subscribed to the conviction popular in his day that a male child was not fully enough developed to have a soul until forty days and that the female fetus could not be judged to have a soul until eighty days, Aquinas condemned abortion at any time, for any reason, because of his beliefs about the dignity of the individual person and the value of human life.

Besides attempting to discredit Aquinas and Augustine, *A Brief, Liberal, Catholic Defense of Abortion* blames "Mariology," or devotion to the Virgin Mary, for what the authors call the Church's "recent" anti-abortion stance. This devotion began when Pope Pius IX defined the Immaculate Conception as a dogma of faith, thus setting the stage for the "holy crusade" against abortion. Dombrowski and Deltete claim that Pius IX reasoned that since the Virgin

Mary was herself conceived immaculately—that is, without sin—then she must have been a "person" from conception. They are especially critical of Pius IX because of his willingness to excommunicate abortionists.

The response to *A Brief, Liberal, Catholic Defense of Abortion* has been predictably split along ideological lines. The pro-life community—especially the Catholic pro-life community—found the book repugnant because it implies that a fetus is, in effect, like vegetation until sentience begins after the twenty-fifth week. The authors assert that performing an abortion on a nonsentient child, therefore, is like mowing the lawn or "pruning a rose bush": "Vegetation has no moral status in the Catholic tradition. A rose bush is neither a moral agent nor a moral patient...the word fetus itself has vegetative connotations, as does abortion, which comes from *abortus,* the suppression of the fruit of the body."[2] Their view is that presentient beings "have no moral standing as moral patients, although they may, as in the case of a fuchsia plant, have indirect moral standing as a result of the fact that they are someone's property."[3] For Dombrowski and Deltete, unborn life is not human life: "A fetus becomes a human being in the moral sense of the term at the same approximate point when it acquires the ability to survive outside the womb."[4]

While most Catholic reviewers found the book reprehensible, many pro-choice advocates lauded it as finally acknowledging the inconsistency and complexity in Church teachings on abortion. One former priest and pro-choice theologian, Anthony Padovano, wrote a glowing review on the Catholics for a Free Choice website, saying, "No book is perfect, but this book is excellent." Noting Dombrowski and Deltete's argument about the Immaculate Conception, Padovano concluded that the authors clearly demonstrate that the reason why the Catholic Church began its "holy crusade against abortion" was only because of misplaced Marian piety and papal loyalty, and because of Pius's reaction against permissive sexuality and feminine autonomy.[5]

It is no accident that such a review, one of the few positive ones, should appear on the website of the Catholics for a Free Choice. For the past three decades, this organization has spent millions of dollars to build a major media presence in an effort to convince the world that Catholics support abortion. With no actual membership—critics routinely refer to the organization as "a well-funded letterhead"—Catholics for a Free Choice was created out of whole cloth by philanthropic institutions with a pro-abortion bias like the Turner Foundation, the Ford Foundation, the David and Lucile Packard Foundation, and the Rockefeller Foundation, as well as Hugh Hefner's Playboy Foundation.[6]

Claiming to speak for the "millions of Catholics who are pro-choice," Frances Kissling, president of Catholics for a Free Choice, argues that she represents the "more than 70% of all Catholics" who do not support the Church's teachings on contraception and abortion. Kissling bills herself as "a former nun," although in fact she left the Sisters of St. Joseph after only six months in the convent, and she acknowledges that today she neither prays nor attends Mass. "For most of my adult life, the Church wasn't particularly relevant to me," she admitted in an interview with *Merge* magazine (an Internet publication). "…I came back as a social change agent." In a 1989 interview with *Mother Jones* magazine, Kissling remarked, "I spent 20 years looking for a government to overthrow without being thrown in jail—I finally found one in the Catholic Church."[7] And so she has devoted most of her career to hammering at the Church. At a roundtable discussion on population issues at the United Nations sponsored by Catholics for a Free Choice in March 1999, she described the Catholic Church as "fatally flawed" and said, "I might have had more success in the Episcopalian Church, where it's not quite so bad, but there are so few Episcopalians, it's not worth it."[8]

In 1970, Kissling operated an abortion clinic in New York, one of two states that allowed abortion at the time. She told the *Washington Post Magazine* in a 1986 interview that her center performed about 30 to 40 abortions each weekday and 70 to 80 on Saturdays.[9] Kissling was also the founder and head of the National Abortion Federation, the professional association for abortion clinics. She contends that there has never been a "Catholic position" on abortion and insists that the Bible proves it. "No one knows when a fetus becomes a human being. The fetus develops as the pregnancy develops—there is a big difference between that one cell on day one and a fetus at twenty-two weeks."[10]

Throughout its organizational materials, including those

geared to teenagers, Catholics for a Free Choice maintains that although the Church may "seem" to teach that abortion is wrong, it is not necessary to pay attention to such teachings. On the Catholics for a Free Choice website, Kissling advises women considering abortion to "weigh all the circumstances in your life and your pregnancy and follow your own conscience. The Catholic Church officially teaches that the conscience of an individual is supreme. If you carefully examine your conscience and then decide that an abortion is the most moral act you can do at this time, you are not committing a sin. Therefore, you are not excommunicated and you do not need to tell it in confession, since in your case, abortion is not a sin."[11] *Conscience,* in fact, is the name of the flagship quarterly magazine of Catholics for a Free Choice.

As part of taking her case to the public, Kissling has spent millions of dollars on advertising for her cause, creating the illusion that she has a constituency among grassroots Catholics as well as among pro-choice foundations. On October 4, 1984, she placed a full-page advertisement in the *New York Times* asserting that there is more than one theologically and ethically defensible viewpoint on abortion within Catholicism and calling for a dialogue among Catholics to acknowledge this "situation of pluralism" in the Church. The ad explicitly asked for the cessation of institutional sanctions against those with dissenting positions on abortion: "Catholics—especially priests, religious, theologians and legislators, who publicly dissent from hierarchical statements and explore areas of moral and legal freedom on the abortion question, should not be penalized by their religious superiors, church employers or bishops."[12] The *New York Times* ad was signed by ninety-seven Catholic scholars, religious and social activists, twenty-four women religious, four priests and brothers, and a large number of lay professors working for Catholic colleges and universities.

One signer, the feminist theologian Elizabeth Schussler-Fiorenza of Harvard Divinity School, moved on from her early days with Catholics for a Free Choice to help unite many of the feminist groups into a coalition called the Women-Church Convergence, "a movement of self-identified women and women-identified men" from all denominations whose common goal is to reinterpret the Gospel from the perspective of women's liberation. Led by Rosemary

Ruether, a theologian at the Garret Evangelical Theological Seminary in Evanston, Illinois, women in the group have created their own life-cycle ceremonies, including rituals to mark the union of lesbian couples and recovery from abortions.[13] A frequent guest speaker on Catholic college campuses, Schussler-Fiorenza pushes the line to undergraduate students that the Catholic Church has always been pluralist when it comes to abortion. She also tells students that she rejects the divinity of Jesus, the true presence of Christ in the Eucharist, and the doctrine of the Trinity, among other fundamental beliefs of the Catholic Church, and that she wants "God" to be replaced by "Goddess."

Women like Elizabeth Schussler-Fiorenza and Frances Kissling are aware that because they are Catholic, they can get away with saying things about the Church that the personnel of NARAL and Planned Parenthood cannot. Most recently, Kissling appropriated a popular devotional image to promote abortion among Hispanic Catholics. In a "prayer card" asking Our Lady of Guadalupe to "keep abortion legal," Kissling uses this figure, revered by Hispanics, to convince them that abortion can be a sacred choice.[14]

Claiming that she simply wants to "reform" the Church and bring it more in line with contemporary thought, Kissling is especially critical of the Vatican and its influence. Decrying its role in encouraging the United Nations to block funding for abortion services, Kissling began a campaign in 1999 to challenge the Vatican's status at the U.N. The Vatican had voluntarily chosen to be a "non-member state permanent observer" so that it would not have to contribute money or take sides in time of war. Catholics for a Free Choice argued that because the Vatican is not a state, it should not be treated as part of the United Nations, even as a permanent observer. "We believe that the Holy See, the government of the Roman Catholic Church, should participate in the United Nations in the same ways as the world's other religions do—as a non-governmental organization."

Operation See Change, as Kissling called her campaign against the Vatican, attempted to persuade the United Nations to revoke the Vatican's status as a permanent observer. "Call it the Holy See, or the Roman Catholic Church, it's a religion, not a country," says the organization's website.[15] Growing from 70 initial endorsers to over

450 pro-abortion organizations worldwide, the See Change Campaign was successful in focusing international public attention on the unique standing of the Vatican at the United Nations. But opposition to the Catholics for a Free Choice initiative was also strong. Senators Rick Santorum (R-PA) and Bob Smith (R-NH) and Representative Chris Smith (R-NJ) introduced congressional resolutions critical of the See Change Campaign and lauding the role of the Vatican at the United Nations. (Kissling dismissed these resolutions as "part of an overall strategy of church conservatives in which a genuine religious commitment to justice is transformed into the worst remnant of state religion—whether manifest in the United Nations, the United States Congress, or United States presidential politics.")[16]

Despite all the publicity that the controversy generated, in the end, not a single member state would sign on to support the Catholics for a Free Choice campaign.[17] But Kissling redefined this failure as a success: "Sometimes it is hard to evaluate the impact of any advocacy effort. Not so, with the See Change Campaign. Aside from the outpouring of support from people and groups from every continent and the media attention it continues to generate, this campaign really seems to have the Vatican worried."[18]

Kissling's work has won her strong support from the pro-choice side. From 1979 to 2000, Catholics for a Free Choice received more than $25 million from private foundations, and lately this figure has been increasing rapidly—especially from its alpha donor, the Ford Foundation, which is deeply involved in funding the organization's pro-choice conferences such as "Catholic Voices: An International Forum on Population and Development." Ford also spent more than $100,000 to help women in developing countries attend an advanced course on feminist perspectives in bioethics at the Kennedy Institute of Ethics, and more than $800,000 for public policy and education programs on reproductive choice in the United States.

The General Service Foundation, like Ford, directly targets the Catholic influence on abortion policy. General Service's aim is "to raise awareness of Catholic support for reproductive health care and to counter the Catholic Church's attempts to undermine reproductive freedom." It also aims "to counter efforts of the Catholic Church to limit legal access to reproductive health care in Latin

America, and to assure participation of pro-choice women's organizations in the debate regarding expansion of legal abortion." Interestingly, James Patrick Shannon, a defrocked Catholic priest and auxiliary bishop of the Archdiocese of St. Paul from 1965 to 1968, sat on the board of directors of the General Service Foundation for many years. Shannon was an outspoken critic of the Church's teachings in the papal encyclical *Humanae Vitae*, and for several years has encouraged General Service to fund programs that strongly counter Church teachings. In recent years, for instance, the foundation has supported International Projects Assistance Services, a manufacturer of manual vacuum-aspiration abortion machines, in its effort to place these devices and train physicians in their use in Ecuador, Nicaragua, and Mexico.[19]

After tracking the finances of Catholics for a Free Choice over several years, Brian Clowes wrote in 2001 that nearly 90 percent of the $1.5 million in direct grants that the organization had distributed over the previous three years had gone to pro-abortion groups in Latin America. About $1.3 million had gone to its own affiliates in Argentina, Bolivia, Brazil, and Mexico.[20] Clowes claims that Catholics for a Free Choice has a strategy of creating confusion, discord, and dissent among Catholics at home and abroad over what the Church actually teaches on abortion. Catholics for a Free Choice knows that if it can gain standing for what it says is the "true" doctrine of the Church—for example, that Catholicism did not always oppose abortion—then the Church will appear inconsistent and punitive when it does oppose abortion.

Indeed, polls show that a majority of Catholic women support the legal right to abortion and a large number believe that it can be a moral decision. The Catholics for a Free Choice website proudly proclaims that 79 percent of U.S. Catholics believe that Catholics should make up their own mind on moral issues like abortion and birth control. In fact, according to the Alan Guttmacher Institute, which tracks reproductive-health data, non-Hispanic Catholic women of childbearing age are 29 percent more likely to have abortions than their Protestant counterparts. Another way of looking at it: while Protestant women make up about 54 percent of the population, they account for only 37 percent of the abortions; Catholic women make up 31 percent of the population and account for 31 percent of the abortions.[21]

Many Catholic politicians have taken note of these figures and continue to assert that they can still be "good" Catholics while supporting a woman's "right to choose." Until recently, few Catholic priests or bishops were willing to confront these politicians, even when the Church's stand on abortion was being publicly misrepresented. But during the 2004 presidential campaign, the Democratic Party's candidate, Senator John Kerry, became what *Catholic Insight* labeled the "lightning rod in the storm" because he not only defended a woman's right to abort her unborn child—even in the latest stages of her pregnancy—but also promised support for assisted suicide, embryonic stem-cell research, and same-sex marriage. All these positions are contrary to the teachings of the Catholic Church.

While Kerry was certainly the most visible pro-choice politician, and therefore the most problematic for the Catholic bishops, many other pro-choice Catholic members of Congress also posed problems. The American Life League counts 71 Catholic members of Congress (out of 150) as reliable pro-abortion voters, and an additional 415 pro-abortion Catholics in state legislatures. These Catholic politicians favor legislation that their Church says they have a "clear and grave obligation to oppose."[22]

By 2004, the situation with elected officials was such that many Catholics began to make unprecedented demands on their bishops to pay attention to the pro-choice politicians within their own dioceses. The first to speak out publicly about whether a pro-choice politician was eligible to receive Communion within the Catholic Church was Archbishop Raymond Burke of St. Louis, who wrote that if Senator Kerry were to present himself for Communion, he would offer a blessing but not the Host. "The archbishop has the right to deny Communion to whomever he wants, but Senator Kerry respectfully disagrees with him on the issue of choice," said Kim Molstre, a Kerry campaign representative. While in St. Louis, Kerry attended a Baptist church.[23]

Kerry attempted to gain additional favor with the pro-choice community by portraying himself as "under siege" by a paternalistic and autocratic Catholic Church. Meanwhile, the media portrayed bishops like Burke as oppressive misogynists. The archbishop acknowledged that speaking the truth was intimidating "because we live, as our Holy Father says, in a culture of death where people want to convince us that everything should be convenient and comfortable. They don't like to hear a voice which says 'this isn't right.' Being outspoken on the truth will bring persecution. Bishops will be persecuted, and also priests and lay people."[24]

During the campaign, Kerry described Church teaching on abortion as a "sectarian" position that has no place in a pluralistic society. In a pastoral letter, Archbishop Burke responded to Kerry by saying that "While the Ten Commandments forbid stealing, no one would believe that laws against theft are an imposition of the Jewish or Christian religions. People of different faiths or of no faith can recognize the natural obligation to respect the property of another. Also, no one would consider Christian opposition to slavery a 'religious' issue. Rather, Christians who oppose slavery and other similar evils are acting according to the standard of right and wrong which has its foundation in our common human nature."[25]

Kerry and other pro-choice Catholic politicians have benefited from what some might regard as the benign neglect practiced by bishops of the past. This hands-off policy carried through the 2004 presidential election season. Archbishop Henry Mansell of Connecticut remained silent on the voting records and rhetoric of pro-choice Catholic politicians while at the same time proactive in working to end the death penalty in his state. Likewise, Cardinal Roger Mahoney of Los Angeles said that the only persons who are to be refused Communion according to Church law are those who have been excommunicated or interdicted, or who obstinately persist in manifestly grave sin. "Since we do not have any of these persons, I am not about to add new sanctions to the reception of Holy Communion." Cardinal Mahoney was joined by a number of other bishops, including Carl Mengeling of Lansing, Michigan, and Howard Hubbard of Albany, New York, as well as Washington's Cardinal Theodore McCarrick.[26]

According to *Catholic Insight*, bishops fall into four categories with respect to Catholic politicians who are pro-choice. The first group includes those like Cardinal Mahoney and Archbishop Mansell, among others, who appear to believe that no public action on the issue is necessary. These bishops hold that the teachings of the Church are clear, and that politicians are adults and hence able to make up their own minds about receiving Communion.

The second group acknowledges that pro-choice politicians are wrong to receive Communion when they support abortion, yet these bishops are unwilling to deny them Communion. Cardinal Francis George of Chicago, Archbishops Tim Dolan of Milwaukee, Charles Chaput of Denver, and Sean O'Malley of Boston, and Bishop John Myers of Newark make up this second group.

A third group of bishops includes those who have taken action against specific politicians. This category includes Bishop William Weigand of Sacramento, who asked Governor Gray Davis to refrain from receiving Communion; and Bishop Robert Carlson of Sioux City, South Dakota, who advised Senator Tom Daschle to stop declaring himself a Catholic until he recanted his pro-abortion stance. Bishops Joseph Galante of Camden, New Jersey, and John Smith of Trenton, New Jersey, advised Governor James McGreevey that they would refuse him Communion because of his support for abortion. Likewise, Bishop Thomas Olmsted of Phoenix rebuked Governor Janet Napolitano for her veto of an informed-consent abortion bill in Arizona.

The fourth group of bishops includes those who believe that abortion is such a grave evil that even ordinary citizens who vote for pro-choice politicians because of their pro-choice stand must themselves refrain from receiving Communion. Among these, in addition to Archbishop Burke of St. Louis, are Bishops Fabian Bruskevitz of Lincoln, Nebraska; Samuel Aquila of Fargo, North Dakota; and Thomas Wenski of Orlando, Florida. Bishop Michael Sheridan of Colorado Springs admonished all Catholics to refrain from receiving Communion if they voted for politicians who support abortion rights, same-sex marriage, euthanasia, or embryonic stem-cell research. In his pastoral letter, Bishop Sheridan wrote that those who make such a political commitment "place themselves outside full communion with the Church and so jeopardize their salvation. Any Catholic who votes for candidates who stand for abortion, illicit stem cell research or euthanasia suffer the same fateful consequences. It is for this reason that these Catholics, whether candidates for office or those who would vote for them, may not receive Holy Communion until they have recanted their positions and been reconciled with God and the Church in the Sacrament of Penance."[27]

Those bishops who publicly challenged pro-choice Catholic politicians were often criticized for contravening the establishment clause of the Constitution. In May 2004, forty-eight Catholic members of Congress, led by Representative Rosa DeLauro (D-CT), signed a letter warning that the Church risked doing serious damage to itself if the bishops decided to withhold Communion from legislators who supported abortion rights or took other public positions at odds with Church doctrine. Written on behalf of Catholic legislators, DeLauro's letter asserted that denying the sacrament in such cases would be "counterproductive and would bring great harm to the Church."[28]

Again in March 2006, Representative DeLauro took the lead in releasing a "Statement of Principals" in which Catholic Democrats in the Congress maintained their pride in being "part of the living Catholic tradition" and said, "We envision a world in which every child belongs to a loving family and agree with the Church about the value of human life and the undesirability of abortion, we do not celebrate its practice." But the statement added, although "we seek the Church's guidance and assistance we believe also in the primacy of conscience."[29] In a news report, one of the fifty-five signers was quoted as saying that the statement arose from frustration at "the way the Church used the Holy Eucharist as a political weapon against some elected officials during the 2004 elections."[30]

The bishops, however, refused to be intimidated. Three top leaders of the U.S. Conference of Catholic Bishops reacted strongly to the statement: Cardinal William Keeler of Baltimore, head of the bishops' Pro-Life Activities Committee; Cardinal Theodore McCarrick of Washington, who heads a task force on Catholic politicians; and Bishop Nicholas DiMarzio of Brooklyn. In their response, they wrote: "While it is always necessary to work to reduce the number of abortions, Catholic teaching calls all Catholics to work actively to restrain, restrict and bring an end to the destruction of unborn human life."[31] The three Catholic leaders reminded the House Catholics that "all Catholics are obliged to shape our consciences in accord with the moral teachings of the Church."[32] Representative DeLauro said that she appreciated the bishops' response, but did not address their rejection of the Catholic lawmakers' request to respectfully disagree with the Church on abortion.[33]

It is difficult to predict where the politics of abortion within Catholicism will lead. But with a new pope who holds an uncompromising attitude on such issues now leading the Church, it is clear that the debates will continue and that they will increasingly be affected by political currents both outside and inside the Church.

CHAPTER EIGHT

Campus Politics of Abortion

AT THE END of the 2005 spring semester—a time when a number of Catholic colleges and universities were hosting pro-abortion commencement speakers and awarding honorary degrees to pro-choice politicians—Stanford Students for Life held their fourth annual Celebrate Life Conference on the Palo Alto campus, and the University of Pennsylvania Students for Life celebrated Respect Life Week 2005 by sponsoring a baby-goods drive at the Penn Law School. Harvard Right to Life held an abortion debate with Harvard Students for Choice, and MIT Pro-Life, which operates under the motto *Because Science Cares*, announced that its group now had 150 members. Meanwhile, Catholic colleges and universities have moved so far from Church teachings on abortion that many of them no longer even make an attempt to nurture a pro-life culture on their own campuses. While the causes for such a retreat from a Catholic identity are complex, the result is clear, if somewhat paradoxical: survey data indicate that support for abortion actually increases for those students attending Catholic colleges and universities—and it increases at a far greater rate than for those Catholic students who attend non-Catholic colleges and universities.

Indeed, two major studies have recently documented that students who attend Catholic universities are more likely to disregard

Church teachings and lose their faith than to retain or enrich it. The Higher Education Research Institute at the University of California, Los Angeles, compared the results of a survey administered to incoming college freshmen in 1997 with a survey given those same students as graduating seniors in 2001. The results indicated a sizeable increase in support for legalized abortion, premarital sex, and same-sex marriage among Catholics about to graduate from Catholic universities.[1] Likewise, an Australian study found that while the majority of the students polled believed that abortion was murder, most said it could be allowed under certain circumstances.[2]

With the release of the Higher Education Research Institute data, liberal Catholic organizations attempted damage control in an effort to prevent further criticism by the Catholic families who send their children to Catholic colleges. Monica Hellwig, then president of the Association of Catholic Colleges and Universities, attempted to put a positive spin on the data: "The real question is whether the task of higher education in our pluralistic, changing society is to lock students into rules—or to teach them critical thinking?" Praising the rejection of "blind obedience," Hellwig did not go on to acknowledge that in order to think critically, students must be taught that there are multiple sides to an issue—and that to use critical thinking, one must learn to apply reason and judgment to understand and evaluate a spectrum of views. Oddly, abortion is rarely debated on Catholic college campuses, either from a reasoned secular viewpoint or from a theological perspective. On some campuses, students are actually encouraged to support abortion, both within the curriculum and in the extracurricular opportunities they participate in.

The Cardinal Newman Society, an orthodox Catholic organization that is trying to help Catholic colleges and universities reclaim their Catholic identity, recently issued a fifty-six-page report entitled "The Culture of Death on Catholic Campuses: A Five Year Review," which documents the pro-choice culture that has emerged on Catholic campuses throughout the country. This study records nearly two hundred instances of campus speakers and honorees who have been public advocates of abortion—including, for example, Pro-Choice America president Kate Michelman, Planned Parenthood president Kim Gandy, and *Hustler* magazine president Larry

Flynt. There are pro-abortion student clubs, including the Reproductive Choice Coalition at Boston College, the Hoyas for Choice at
Georgetown University, and Georgetown Students for Choice at
the Georgetown Law School.[3]

In addition to hearing from abortion advocates, students on
many Catholic campuses are encouraged to become directly involved
in supporting the abortion industry by participating in internships
at organizations such as Planned Parenthood. At Nazareth College's
campus ministry program, students can volunteer as "clinic escorts"
to women pursuing abortions at Planned Parenthood. At Villanova
University and at DePaul University in Chicago, students may also
intern with Planned Parenthood. Likewise, Georgetown University,
which describes itself as "the nation's oldest Catholic and Jesuit university," provides a link to Planned Parenthood on its website, and,
like other Catholic colleges, suggests the use of the abortifacient
morning-after pill.[4] Santa Clara University in California, which was
founded by the Jesuits in 1851, not only links to Planned Parenthood
on its medical-assistance website, but also informs students that this
organization "provides services including family planning, pregnancy
testing, prenatal care, cancer screening, surgical sterilization and
abortion." At Seattle University, students are directed through the
university's website to Planned Parenthood and are urged to consider
"activism" with groups including the pro-choice National Organization for Women and the National Gay and Lesbian Task Force.

Sometimes, pro-choice speakers are invited to campus as part
of an attempt to link abortion rights to the greater Catholic commitment to social justice. As the keynote speaker for their annual
"Social Issues Conference" a few years ago, the University of San
Diego invited Morris Dees, cofounder of the Southern Poverty Law
Center. Dees, who has helped fund the abortion clinic operated by
his wife, Mary Farmer, has used his position at the Southern Poverty
Law Center to link anti-abortion politics to abortion-clinic violence
by filing lawsuits against pro-life groups.

Some students have reacted by forming "Students for Life"
organizations at the University of San Diego and other campuses,
but pro-life students must compete with other, sometimes more popular student organizations for scarce funding—and they often lose
out. At USD, a board composed of representatives from the Associ-

ated Students makes recommendations on funding for student groups. Some of these student representatives, including those from the gay and lesbian community and the women's center, are openly hostile to the pro-life position. Unlike the gay and lesbian student group on campus, the pro-life students are given no dedicated office or space to meet. Throughout the academic year 2004–2005, the beleaguered organization met in the dorm bedroom of the pro-life club president. Likewise, pro-life campus speakers are often marginalized or ignored. A few years ago, an internationally known figure in the pro-life movement, Fr. Paul Marx, the founder of Human Life International, addressed a nearly empty auditorium on the San Diego campus. There had been little publicity about the event and most students were unaware of Fr. Marx's impending visit. A few pro-life faculty and secretarial support staff members were in attendance, along with a handful of students, but no academic administrators. By contrast, when the Communist activist Angela Davis visited the San Diego campus, she received accolades from administrators and faculty alike. Professors gave extra credit to students who attended her lecture on radical politics, a woman's right to choose, and embracing a lesbian identity.

A few years ago, the American Association of University Professors held a national conference at the University of San Diego to discuss the threats to academic freedom on Catholic campuses. Acting like "freedom fighters" arriving to help stem a new Catholic Inquisition, panels advised faculty that they certainly owed no allegiance to the Catholic Church itself, nor should they temper their teaching to conform to "official" Catholic doctrine. But most faculty and administrators did not need this reassurance. While Pope John Paul II made an attempt to ensure that at least the courses in Catholic theology reflect authentic Church teaching, the reality is that many Catholic campuses are Catholic in name only.

Few Catholic parents are aware of this situation. George Weigel has responded to this sea change by asking: "What about consumer fraud? If some Catholic colleges and universities have become venues in which Catholic students stop thinking and living like Catholics, something is desperately awry." Weigel also reminds Catholic theologians teaching on Catholic campuses of *Ex Corde Ecclesiae*, the 1990 papal statement on Catholic higher education. In this statement, Pope John Paul II defined what it means to be a Catholic college by applying canon law and authorized bishops to determine which colleges can be declared "Catholic." *Ex Corde* identifies the "dignity of human life" as foremost among serious contemporary problems that ought to be studied in Catholic colleges. The Cardinal Newman Society's "Culture of Death" report points out that "It is in one of its General Norms that *Ex Corde Ecclesiae* provides the clearest instruction to Catholic colleges that make accommodations for the Culture of Death: Catholic teaching and discipline are to influence all university activities."[5]

Vatican officials have recently implied that Pope Benedict XVI is ready to act on the matter of Catholic colleges and their adherence to the faith. Early in 2006, the Vatican's second education official in command, Archbishop Michael Miller, secretary of the Vatican Congregation for Catholic Education, predicted that the pope will follow a path of "evangelical pruning" of secularized Catholic colleges and universities, pronouncing them to be no longer Catholic.[6] (Most recently, the Archdiocese of New York responded to the Cardinal Newman Society's protest of Marist College's commencement speaker, the pro-choice Eliot Spitzer, by declaring that the college "is no longer a Catholic institution.")[7]

On some campuses, administrators are beginning to take action. The president of Trinity College in Vermont revoked a speaking invitation issued to the pro-abortion feminist Gloria Steinem. The president of Gonzaga University canceled a lecture by a Planned Parenthood representative organized by a women's studies student club. Officials at Christian Brothers University in Memphis disinvited the Reverend James Lawson, an abortion-rights advocate who had been invited to campus by Pax Christi, the Catholic peace group on campus. Women's studies professors at the College of the Holy Cross canceled a lecture by Frances Kissling of Catholics for a Free Choice after the college president refused to pay Kissling's speaking fee and criticized the women's studies staff for its poor judgment. Catholic University of America canceled a planned book signing by Eleanor Holmes Norton, a pro-abortion politician.[8] At Providence College in Rhode Island, when three students posted abortion-rights fliers throughout the campus featuring an image of the Virgin Mary and the message "How's this for an immaculate concept: Keep Abortion Safe and Legal," the college president, the Reverend Philip Smith, called the incident a "deliberate misuse of a venerated person" and suspended the students involved.

Activist alumni groups have also attempted to take a stand. When Chris Matthews, the host of MSNBC's *Hardball*, was invited to give the commencement address at the College of the Holy Cross, the alumni leaders angrily noted that Matthews has publicly advocated abortion rights during his television appearances and in his newspaper columns. (While claiming to be "personally opposed" to abortion, Matthews has declared himself "pro-choice" and has also expressed sympathy for supporters of partial-birth abortion in cases of severely handicapped babies.) In response to Matthews' invitation to campus, Bishop Daniel Reilly of Worcester, Massachusetts, canceled his participation in the commencement ceremony, and the alumni began a drive to withhold donations until Holy Cross strengthened its Catholic identity.

Beyond the established Catholic colleges and universities, more than a dozen new or planned Roman Catholic institutions have emerged after a period of twenty-five years in which no new Catholic colleges were established. These more traditional Catholic colleges, such as Franciscan University in Steubenville, Ohio, and Ave Maria in Naples, Florida, have a strong pro-life commitment already integrated into their academic culture. In a recent article in the *Chronicle of Higher Education,* the Reverend Joseph D. Fessio, a Jesuit and Ave Maria's chancellor, commented that "Many Catholic institutions have ceased to be places where the fullness of Catholic truth is joyfully and vigorously taught, defended and proclaimed." At Ave Maria, on the other hand, Mass is celebrated three times a day and Latin is a required subject. Every evening a group of students and faculty members gather for what Ave Maria calls a "rosary walk" proclaiming the twenty mysteries of the life of Jesus Christ.[9] Ave Maria students have provided food and gifts to migrant farm workers' children, and have also provided sidewalk counseling to women seeking abortion at a local abortion clinic each Friday.

SECULAR COLLEGES STEP INTO THE BREACH

While Catholic campuses have struggled with their identity, pro-life students on secular campuses are paradoxically becoming more organized than ever, as was seen by their involvement in the 2004 presidential election. As the campaigns heated up, Princeton University's daily paper, the *Daily Princetonian,* published an article sponsored by Princeton Pro-Life. The article called on readers to "unite in identifying the war against the unborn as the graver evil" in the upcoming federal elections and reminded students that "with the major election approaching, we must reflect upon two critical issues: abortion and embryo-destructive research.... A vote for a pro-abortion/embryo destruction candidate is a vote for the direct and intentional killing of innocent human beings." The author also argued that killing an embryonic human being to harvest stem cells is just as evil as killing a mentally handicapped child to harvest organs for transplant: "It is time to put away tired clichés. You cannot be personally opposed to abortion while thinking others should have the choice. You may as well be personally opposed to slavery but in support of others having the choice to own slaves. In the case of abortion, that choice is a choice for murder."[10]

There were similar episodes at other schools. A coalition of pro-life student organizations from fourteen elite colleges and universities published the same pro-life advertisement in their student newspapers on the same day, October 19, 2004. Entitled "Human Rights for All," it asked readers to withhold their support from politicians who "deny basic human rights to an entire class of human beings" and reminded them that "a vote for a pro-embryo-destruction candidate is a vote for the direct and intentional killing of innocent human beings." The advertisements were purchased by pro-life student organizations at each of the participating institutions, including Princeton, Yale, Harvard, Cornell, the University of Pennsylvania, Dartmouth, Stanford, the University of Virginia, Columbia, New York University, Georgetown, the Massachusetts Institute of Technology, Notre Dame, Johns Hopkins, and the University of California at Berkeley. With the exception of Notre Dame and Georgetown, all of these schools are secular.[11]

Invoking science rather than religion, the pro-life organization at the Massachusetts Institute of Technology defines itself as being devoted to "fostering respect for human life from the moment of conception until natural death, and to promoting educational support for the pro-life position." The group's goal is to "be a resource for MIT students to examine in-depth the social, medical and legal aspects of the pro-life response to abortion and euthanasia."[12] In the past, MIT Pro-Life has sponsored debates, speakers, information booths on campus, and joint events with other collegiate pro-life groups, including the National Pro-Life March in Washington, D.C., and volunteer work for pro-life pregnancy help centers.

Like MIT Pro-Life, the Dartmouth Coalition for Life claims: "The convenient but misleading conservative/liberal, Republican/Democratic, reactionary/progressive classifications cannot adequately describe our group as a whole. Our members can and do disagree on many other issues. All are brought together, however, through their belief in three principles which we aim to promote and support in the Dartmouth community and beyond: We believe that human life is precious. We believe that human life begins at conception. We believe in the fundamental right to life."[13] The organization's website provides pro-life articles written by Dartmouth students as well as links to a number of pro-life organizations and the Ivy League Coalition for Life, a nondenominational coalition of pro-life groups from universities and colleges in the northeastern United States.

Harvard Right to Life, a part of the Ivy League Coalition for Life, provides a forum for discussion about the right to life and assists students who wish to opt out of paying the portion of the University Health Services fee that funds abortions. Harvard Right to Life members also perform volunteer work with pregnancy centers in Boston. In 2005, students from the organization participated in a debate with representatives of the Harvard Students for Choice. The *Harvard Crimson* reported that the debate opened with five-minute statements from each side, followed by a rotation of one-minute responses and rebuttals. After an hour of debate, both teams invited questions from the audience, most of which addressed ethical issues surrounding abortion. According to the *Crimson* report, the pro-life students wrestled with these questions while those on the pro-choice side "refused to do so, saying they only wanted to discuss the legal aspects of abortion." One student who attended the event complained, "I was surprised that the pro-choice side refused to address the moral side of the debate. I thought they could have addressed it in a much better fashion."[14]

Pro-life students at Stanford, Columbia, Princeton, Harvard, Yale, MIT, Brown, the University of Chicago, Penn, and other campuses have access to a growing support network of pro-life organizations, including Feminists for Life and American Collegians for Life—a student-run, nonprofit group that is the nation's oldest pro-life organization wholly devoted to educating college students about the medical and ethical issues of abortion, euthanasia, and infanticide. Since 1987, the group has worked to develop a nation-wide network of pro-life students. Now connecting hundreds of college campuses in the largest national directory of its kind, American Collegians for Life has grown substantially during the past few years. Its 2005 conference, held at Catholic University of America's Columbus School of Law, educated and trained more than 350 students, representing more than 70 universities, on various life issues. One heavily attended workshop was called "Thinking Globally, Acting Locally: How to Build a Campus Culture of Life," while another described the feminist role in creating a culture of life.[15]

In interviews with the pro-life students at elite U.S. colleges and universities, *City Journal*'s Brian C. Anderson found many students like Nikki McArthur, a senior at Yale who is "ardently pro-life" though not because she believes that "an embryo is a full human being." Rather, she told Anderson, "I think that a culture in which abortion is widely accepted is one in which people have a wrong understanding of children and sex. Children should not be considered burdens." At Princeton, Anderson interviewed twenty-five students who shared similar views on cultural issues. He described one of them, Jordan Rodriguez, as "a rugged-looking Evangelical Princeton undergrad, Deke pledge president, and hyperachiever." In his San Antonio high school, Rodriguez was a member of the varsity baseball team, editor of the literary magazine at his school, and a violist in the city's Youth Philharmonic—and he "is as hard line as they come on abortion." Rodriguez told Anderson, "The practice [of abortion] is ethically abominable; it should be regarded as a form of homicide and prosecuted as such."[16]

Anderson also found that the number of College Republicans has almost tripled in the past six years, from 400 or so campus chapters to 1,148 today, with 120,000-plus members. (In comparison, there are around 900 chapters of College Democrats, with 100,000 members.) At Princeton, the College Republican group has doubled in size over the past few years, to more than 400 students. At the University of Pennsylvania, the number of College Republicans has jumped from 25 to more than 700 today. Many of these college-age Republicans are pro-life. In fact, a poll by the UCLA Higher Education Research Institute found that support for abortion has declined dramatically among college-age students. In the early 1990s, two-thirds of all students supported abortion; now it is barely half.

The pro-life student iconoclasts must contend with a generally liberal agenda among student-affairs administrators—who are more likely to schedule a celebration of *Roe v. Wade* or hold a "Take Back the Night" rally to protest date rape than to help organize a pro-life fundraising activity—and with faculty members who hold the pro-life position in contempt.

During the spring of 2006, there were several incidents of vandalism against pro-life campus displays. The first of these occurred on April 12, 2006, when a tenured professor at Northern Kentucky University led a number of her graduate students to destroy a pro-life display on her campus. Professor Sally Jacobsen was photographed stomping on and destroying a campus-approved exhibit that included approximately four hundred small white crosses meant to represent a cemetery for aborted fetuses. Professor Jacobsen, using Orwellian logic, characterized her role in the destruction of property as an "exercise of her freedom of speech.... I did, outside of class during the break, invite students to express their freedom of speech rights to destroy the display if they wished to." She justified her actions on the basis of the outrage that she and some of her students felt at seeing the display, which she called a "slap in the face" to women contemplating abortion.[17]

Later that same month, in what the *Daily Princetonian* described as an "incident of politically motivated vandalism," the Princeton Pro-Life flag display in front of the Frist Campus Center was destroyed. The 347 flags had been erected to represent the lives of students who might have become members of Princeton's Class of 2010 had abortion not been legalized. The flags were pulled out of the ground, and coat hangers were strewn all around. In addition, the sign in front of the display was trampled and in its place were put signs reading: "Support small class sizes: support abortion," and "347 rusty coat hangers were saved from mangling and mutilation."[18]

In a similar campus incident just a few weeks later, a pro-life club's poster exhibit at Western Washington University was destroyed by a male student who was photographed and videotaped as he tore down the entire display. At one point he picked up one of the plastic pipes used as framework and hurled it through a poster, ripping it to shreds. When he had completed the destruction, the student left the enclosure and rejoined a handful of pro-abortion supporters who had gathered to cheer him on.[19]

Despite these incidents, the politics of abortion on college campuses—both Catholic and secular—is taking on odd and unforeseen shapes as formerly monolithic positions break down and conventional wisdom is challenged.

CHAPTER NINE

Signs of Life

A FEW YEARS AGO, in the middle of an episode of the television series *Friends*, a remarkable commercial appeared. Strategically placed during the broadcast of the most-anticipated episode of the season, in which a main character on the show was scheduled to give birth, the commercial introduced General Electric's 4D Ultrasound imaging system, a new development in prenatal ultrasound technology. Correctly predicting a large audience of young female viewers, the sponsors of the commercial opened with the haunting refrain from Roberta Flack's song "The First Time Ever I Saw Your Face," then seductively drew the viewer's attention to a computer screen in a hospital room with a glowing ultrasound image of an unborn child. The camera angle then widened to focus on the expectant parents—the mother and father gazing longingly at the golden image of their unborn baby as he sucked his thumb, kicked his legs, and appeared to float in an almost magical world. The image was galvanizing for viewers and was the subject of much comment after its premiere.

The 4D imaging system brings the fourth dimension to ultrasound, offering clear, moving, three-dimensional pictures of the unborn child in real time. The response to this capability has been tremendous, and has had a significant impact on the politics of abortion. Expectant parents are demanding the new technology from their obstetricians, who have rushed to purchase the expensive machines for their offices. To meet the growing demand, savvy entrepreneurs have opened 4D Ultrasound imaging centers at shopping malls throughout the country so that expectant parents can enter the world of their unborn child. Satisfied customers are effusive in their praise for the technology on the GE website. One mother wrote, "I even think I saw him smile." Another said that the images "made me feel so close to my baby, it actually made me cry."

General Electric's 4D Ultrasound commercial was so powerful that the pro-choice side had to respond. The liberal *American Prospect Online* criticized GE for even making the commercial in an article entitled "They Bring Good Spin to Life." Labeling the commercial "propaganda," author Matthew Nisbet called the ad a "milieu of clever illusion that blurs the distinction between a fetus and a newborn infant."[1] But of course this "blurring" is the heart of the matter, having been at the core of the pro-life position for decades and having been the issue for many philosophers, theologians, and bioethics scholars who have long asserted that there is no substantial change between the unborn child and the newborn infant.

Robert P. George, the McCormick Professor of Jurisprudence and director of the James Madison Program in American Ideals and Institutions at Princeton University, has written persuasively about this biological and philosophical continuity. He maintains that "the development of a human being from the zygotic stage of its existence to the adult stage is the development of a distinct, unitary substance. At no point in its development was the human being that now is an adult a different substance, being or thing than he or she is currently." Using the phrase in its accepted philosophical sense, Professor George simply states that there is no "substantial" change—the being in the womb is a human being, the same human being from conception onward.[2]

Some on the radical fringe of the pro-choice movement accept George's views on human development but argue perversely that if there is no substantial change from the preborn to the newborn infant, and since the law already permits the killing of the preborn, it follows that there is nothing to stop a parent from killing his newborn child if the presence of that child will impose an undue burden on the family. One of those who hold this position is Peter Singer, another Princeton professor and longtime supporter of abortion rights. In *Writings on an Ethical Life,* Singer argues that the life of the fetus is of no greater value than the life of a nonhuman animal at a similar level of rationality, self-consciousness, and capacity for feeling. Like most pro-choice advocates, he believes that "no fetus has the same claim to life as a person." But unlike mainstream pro-choice advocates, he carries this assumption to its logical extreme in defense of infanticide: "It must be admitted that these arguments apply to the newborn baby as much as to the fetus. A week-old baby is not a rational and self conscious being, and there are many non-human animals whose rationality, self consciousness, awareness, and capacity to feel, exceed that of a human baby a week or a month old." Singer complains that we erroneously believe, "because infants are cute, that we should be more concerned about killing them." He goes on to say that we need to "put aside feelings based on the small, helpless, and sometimes, cute appearance of human infants. To think that the lives of infants are of special value because infants are small and cute is on par with thinking that a baby seal, with its soft fur and large round eyes, deserves greater protection than a gorilla, who lacks these attributes.... If we can put aside these emotionally moving but strictly irrelevant aspects of the killing of a baby, we can see that the grounds for not killing persons do not apply to new-born infants."[3]

Singer cites historical precedent to support his views: "In some societies, infanticide was not merely permitted, but in certain circumstances, it was deemed morally obligatory. Not to kill a deformed or sickly infant was often regarded as wrong, and infanticide was probably the first, and in several societies, the only, form of population control." Responding to critics who view such practices as "uncivilized," he says: "We might think that we are just more 'civilized' than these primitive people. But it is not easy to feel confident that we are more civilized than the best Greek and Roman moralists. It was not just the Spartans who exposed their infants on hillsides: both Plato and Aristotle recommended the killing of deformed infants."[4]

For Singer, there is nothing intrinsically wrong with infanticide—just as there is nothing intrinsically wrong with abortion.

Because she is an adult human being, the woman's needs always take precedence. In a recent interview published in *WORLD* magazine, Singer elaborated on his views: infanticide should be permitted with born children who are ill or who have ill older siblings in need of their body parts. *WORLD* interviewer Marvin Olasky asked, "What about parents conceiving and giving birth to a child specifically to kill him, take his organs and transplant them into their ill older children?" Singer responded, "It is difficult to warm to parents who can take such a detached view, but they are not doing something wrong in itself." Asked if there would be anything wrong with a society in which children were bred for spare parts on a massive scale, Singer replied, "No." Asked if it would be ethically acceptable to kill a one-year-old child with physical or mental disabilities, Singer responded in the affirmative.[5]

People who are appalled by such thinking may comfort themselves by saying that Singer speaks only for the most radical edge of the pro-choice side, but he certainly is not treated like a marginal figure. He enjoys a prestigious position with high status and a generous salary at Princeton University as the distinguished DeCamp Professor of Bioethics. When he was appointed, not a single member of the current Princeton faculty, with the exception of Robert George, publicly spoke out against him or his long-documented and highly publicized defense of infanticide and euthanasia. Opposition to Singer's appointment has come almost entirely from outside the university community. As Professor George writes, "Among orthodox secularists at Princeton and elsewhere, Singer's appointment at Princeton is uncontroversial."[6]

Friends like Peter Singer who accept the "blurring of the boundaries" have turned out to be the abortion-rights movement's worst enemies. The idea that the fetus and the child are biologically unconnected is the movement's core belief, and this explains why pro-choice activists immediately took aim at General Electric's 4D Ultrasound commercial that allows viewers to enter into the world of the unborn.

General Electric responded to this criticism by changing its website's published testimonials from parents, deleting those that spoke of "bonding" with the unborn child. Eventually, GE withdrew the television ad altogether. Parents' testimonials on the website now focus on the developmental and diagnostic benefits offered by the imaging. One parent simply comments that it was good to see that her twins were developing on schedule, while another dispassionately says that the technology diagnosed a cleft palate and "allowed us to prepare for the delivery rather than being shocked at the birth." All emotionally charged terms like "our baby" are gone. Responding to the pro-choice criticism that the ads made the fetus look too much like a "child," General Electric now offers a caveat on its website: "The American Institute of Ultrasound in Medicine advocates the responsible use of diagnostic ultrasound. The AIUM strongly discourages the non-medical use of ultrasound for psychosocial or entertainment purposes."[7]

Pro-choice advocates know that before the new 4D technology, it was easier to maintain that because there is no agreement about the beginning of human life, abortion is a privacy issue—a personal religious or philosophical decision. Old-school liberal politicians like New York's Mario Cuomo, who recently appeared on NBC's *Meet the Press* to suggest that "we form a committee of scientists and ethicists to find out when life really begins," continue to insist that a fetus is a "potential" human being, not an unborn child, and that it is a woman's right, even in pregnancy, to hold dominion over her body.[8] Such politicians would require that all medical students involved in an obstetrics and gynecology rotation receive training in abortion procedures, and have demanded draconian rules curtailing the right to assembly for pro-life prayer, protests, and sidewalk counseling near abortion facilities. They have even tried to use the law to stifle the science of the sonograms.

For instance, New York State's attorney general, Eliot Spitzer, not long ago attempted to block anti-abortion "crisis pregnancy centers" from implementing the ultrasound technology in their own facilities. Spitzer issued thirty-four subpoenas to centers throughout the state of New York "suspected of deceiving women about their services or practicing medicine without a license." One of the "subversive activities" that these centers were allegedly engaged in was simply providing pregnancy counseling coupled with ultrasound imaging to expectant mothers. Working closely with Family Planning Advocates of New York State, an umbrella group that includes seventy-eight family-planning clinics and abortion facilities, including

fifteen operated by Planned Parenthood, Spitzer claimed to be prob-
ing complaints that the groups "lure women with the promise of
reproductive health services, only to present them with anti-abortion
messages."[9]

Spitzer issued subpoenas demanding that the centers provide
his office with copies of all advertisements, website addresses, services
provided, names of staff members, training materials, and blank
forms and records of all agreements made. Working closely with
Spitzer in the campaign against the pro-life crisis pregnancy centers,
JoAnn Smith, president and chief executive officer of Family Planning Advocates, warned that "a new trend at the centers is to offer
sonograms." The ultrasound technology especially concerned Smith
because she claimed that the centers "lack the medical personnel
and licenses necessary to provide the service correctly.... We are not
trying to close down the facilities, but we take seriously a woman's
right to reproductive services." The fact that all this legalese masked
an effort to close these facilities down was revealed by the NARAL
Pro-Choice America website, featuring a program in which they ask
women to participate in undercover sting operations designed to
"expose the true nature and tactics of deceptive crisis pregnancy
centers."

While Spitzer was successful in making service provision more
difficult for the crisis pregnancy centers, it is hard to stop a medical
technology in a free market. And it is hard to stop women's reactions
to images of their unborn children. The *New York Times* recently
published a front-page report on the use of ultrasound technology in
crisis pregnancy centers throughout the country. Author Neela
Banerjee introduced *Times* readers to women who had visited these
centers with the intention of getting an abortion, but changed their
minds once they saw the ultrasound images. Banerjee tells about
one of these women:

> Sixteen months ago, Andrea Brown, 24 years old and unmarried, was
> desperate for an abortion, fearing the disappointment of her parents
> and the humiliation she might face. While frantically searching the
> telephone book one day, she came across the Bowie Crofton Preg-
> nancy Center and Medical Clinic, a church financed organization
> that provides counseling and education about sexual abstinence. As
> they are required to do, the Bowie receptionist told Ms. Brown on the

telephone when she first called that the clinic did not perform abortions or make referrals for abortion, but offered to make an appointment so that Brown could come in for an ultrasound to make sure her six and a half week pregnancy was viable. When she did, everything changed.[10]

Places like the Bowie Center are on the front lines in the struggle over abortion, and so they have taken hits. The *New York Times* reported that on the eve of the 2005 anniversary of *Roe v. Wade,* the windows of the Bowie Center were smashed and its walls were spray-painted with graffiti, including the word "choice." Complaining that the treatment of women who visit crisis pregnancy centers is "coercive," Susanne Martinez, vice president of public policy at Planned Parenthood Federation of America, told the *New York Times,* "From the time they walk into these centers, they are inundated with information that is propaganda and that has one goal in mind. And that is to have women continue with their pregnancies."[11] The Bowie Center's director, Pam Palumbo, responded that changing a mind is not the same as coercion. About 45 percent of the women who test positive for pregnancy at the facility are "abortion-minded," she said; it is the use of ultrasound technology that has "convinced 50 to 75 percent of these women to change their minds."

Fearful that the pro-life perspective will deter women from getting abortions, the Feminist Women's Health Center, a group that operates abortion clinics in several states, warns women on its website that they should stay away from crisis pregnancy centers altogether: "If you discover you are seeking help from an anti-abortion facility, protect yourself from further harassment. Leave the premises immediately and do not return. When you do locate a professional clinic that offers information about all options, be sure to share your experience with your new counselor so that whatever distortions and misinformation you may have received can be corrected."[12]

Despite the attempts by abortion-rights advocates to suppress the technology, however, the widespread use of ultrasound has created a society that is "more fetally aware," according to Professor David Garrow of the Emory Law School. "Baby's first picture is now routinely tacked to the refrigerator door before baby is even born, reflecting feelings that are more conflicted than many abortion rights activists acknowledge."[13] The language of choice that defines abortion as simply "expelling a cluster of cells" is uncomfortably inconsistent with what women see by their own eyes. As the anecdotal evidence from the crisis pregnancy centers reveals, technology reduces the rate of abortion. More than a decade ago, before the availability of 4D imaging, a study published in the *New England Journal of Medicine* provided additional evidence for the power of ultrasound technology in changing women's hearts and minds— even women who thought they had no doubts about their decision to abort. The journal reported that when pregnant women came to an abortion clinic and were shown ultrasound pictures of the fetus before the abortion, only one out of ten went through with the procedure.[14]

In addition to changing the minds of those seeking abortion, ultrasound technology has also changed the hearts and minds of an increasing number of abortion-service providers, too. One of the founders of the National Abortion Rights Action League in 1968, Bernard Nathanson had not only presided over sixty thousand abortions, but performed thousands himself—including the abortion of his own child. Yet once he began using ultrasound, Nathanson found himself "bonding with the unborn." He renounced his abortion advocacy and became a pro-life advocate: "When ultrasound in the early 1970s confronted me with the sight of the embryo in a womb, I simply lost my faith in abortion on demand."[15]

Nathanson attempted to express some of the ambivalence he was feeling about abortion in an article for the *New England Journal of Medicine* in 1974, just a year after the *Roe v. Wade* decision for which he had lobbied so long. As he recalls, "It was not a pro-life article but in it I articulated my growing doubts and fears about what I had been doing. I made the flat statement that although I had presided over thousands of deaths I began to see that the fetus is life." Even in 1974, Nathanson began to believe: "There is no longer serious doubt in my mind that human life exists within the womb from the very onset of pregnancy, despite the fact that the nature of intrauterine life has been the subject of considerable dispute in the past." He also warned doctors: "We must courageously face the fact, finally, that human life of a special order is being taken in the process of abortion.... [A]bortion must be seen as the interruption of a process which would otherwise have produced a citizen of the world."[16]

The reader response to Nathanson's article was the largest ever received by the *New England Journal of Medicine*. Nathanson says that the journal's editors were "deluged by mail and they sent them all to me.... These letters were not fan letters. They were coming from physicians who had excoriated me for being an abortionist just four years earlier but now, as the abortion pie had grown and they were pulling in the money right and left, they had changed their minds about abortion. I was overwhelmed by the vituperation, the threats, and the phone calls. Threats were made against my life and my family." But Nathanson had stepped over his own private Rubicon: "Having looked at the ultrasound, I could no longer go on as before."

Other abortion providers changed their minds not so much because of ultrasound as because of the realization that what they were doing, stripped of the political rationalizations, was taking human life. Dr. Anthony Levitano learned to do abortions as part of his medical training and continued to provide abortion services to his patients for eight years. All along he had to suppress subversive thoughts: "As a doctor, you know that these are children; you know that these are human beings with arms and legs and heads and they move around and they are very active. But you get reminded—and you need to be reminded—every time you put that scanner down on somebody's uterus—you are reminded. Because you see a child in there—hearts beating, arms flinging." It was only when Levitano and his wife began trying to conceive their own child and had difficulty that he began to reconsider his involvement in abortion. "We had been married for a few years—and no baby. Suddenly, we realized we had an infertility problem. I kept doing abortions. But it was tough. We started desperately looking for a baby to adopt, and here I was throwing them in the garbage at a rate of nine and ten a week. It even occurred to me then: I wish one of these people would just let me have their child. But it doesn't work that way. So the conflict was there."

Dr. Levitano and his wife were eventually successful in adopting a child, and everything seemed fine. But a few years later, their child was hit by a car and killed. This tragedy altered Levitano's perspective.

> When you lose a child, your child, your life is very different. Everything changes. All of a sudden the idea of a person's life becomes very real. It is not an embryology course anymore. It is not just a couple of hundred dollars. It is the real thing. It is your child you buried. After a few months, I started to realize—this is somebody's child. I lost my child, someone who was precious to us. And now I am taking somebody's child and I am tearing him right out of the womb. I am killing somebody's child.... I began to feel like a paid assassin. It wasn't worth it to me anymore. It was costing me too much personally. All the money in the world would not have made a difference.[17]

The gradual realization that "human life" was being taken in an abortion also drew Dr. Beverly McMillan away from the practice. Though raised in a conservative Christian home in Tennessee, McMillan had "adopted the ideology of radical pro-abortion feminism" as a young medical student. Then, as a new physician, she went on to open what soon became the largest abortion clinic in the state of Mississippi.[18]

After five successful years building her clinic, McMillan began to experience misgivings:

> One of the things that began to bother me was when I would do the suction D & C procedure, I would go over to the suction bottle and go outside the room to a sink where I would personally pick through it with a forceps. I would have to identify the four extremities, the spine, the skull and the placenta. If I didn't find that, I would have to go back and scrape and suction some more, or else my patients would be showing up in 48 or 72 hours with problems. Standing at that sink, I guess I just started seeing these bodies for the first time. I don't know what I did before that. I think I just counted. Blood didn't make me sick. I could handle all the guts and gore of medicine. But I started seeing this for the first time and it started bothering me.[19]

For Joan Appleton, head nurse at the Commonwealth Women's Clinic in Washington, D.C., and formerly an active member of NOW, it was a "troubling ultrasound abortion" that helped her recognize that what she was aborting was a living child: "I han-

SIGNS OF LIFE   *131*

dled the ultrasound while the doctor performed the procedure and I directed him while I was watching the screen. I saw the baby pull away. I saw the baby open his mouth. I had seen *Silent Scream,* but it hadn't affected me.* To me it was just more pro-life propaganda. But, I couldn't deny what I saw on the screen. After that procedure I was shaking, literally, but managed to pull it together and continue on with the day."

While shaken, Appleton kept on providing abortion services. Rationalizing that she was helping women achieve equality with men, Appleton "began to work more closely with Planned Parenthood and the National Abortion Rights League on certain projects.... I started out in the pro-choice movement believing that I was helping women, believing that women had a right to choose. Women had a right to life. They had a right to go on. I thought when I was counseling women, I was helping them through a difficult situation so they could go on with their lives. I told each woman she was the most important person on this earth and that once this was over she could go on with her life."

But the women she counseled were just getting pregnant again and having abortions again. Appleton began to resent them and then to pity them.[20] "Why was abortion such an emotional trauma for women?...Why are they coming back to me months and years later—psychological wrecks?" Appleton had no one to talk with about these questions: "I couldn't go to a feminist leader like Molly Yard and say, 'Molly, you got a minute?'" But there was one anti-abortion sidewalk counselor at her clinic, Debra Braun, whom Appleton trusted because she saw that Braun cared about women. Appleton struck up an acquaintance. The two had many conversations over several years. They became good friends and eventually Appleton left her clinic. Later, she worked with Braun at Pro-Life Action Ministries, where her assignment was to help troubled staff leave abortion clinics as she had and achieve reconciliation and healing.[21]

---

*In 1984, Bernard Nathanson helped create the film *Silent Scream,* which depicted the sonogram image of a twelve-week-old fetus being aborted by the combination of suction and crushing instrumentation. The only national showing of the graphic film—widely denounced by the pro-choice side—was on the Public Broadcasting System's *Frontline* program in 1985.

While the journey from the pro-choice position to the pro-life position was unique for each provider, most shared the realization that they were part of an industry involved in taking human life. This realization emerged gradually—sometimes assisted by ultrasound technology, family tragedy, or the visual reminder that an unborn baby's life had been taken; but when it did emerge, it brought a compelling epiphany. Crucial to many conversions were the pro-life sidewalk counselors at abortion facilities, whose "rescues" sometimes involve ambivalent abortion providers themselves. Sensing the danger that these counselors pose, Planned Parenthood has forbidden their clinic employees from even talking with them.[22]

The sympathetic understanding of the pro-life sidewalk counselors was one of the main reasons that Norma McCorvey, the "Jane Roe" plaintiff in *Roe v. Wade,* moved to the pro-life position. Mary Meehan writes that "McCorvey was working in a Texas abortion clinic when Reverend Flip Benham of Operation Rescue moved in next door. Years later, Benham and the little daughter of an Operation Rescue worker both befriended 'Miss Norma.'" Soon Benham baptized McCorvey, who joined the anti-abortion movement. Although she was unsuccessful in her attempt to petition the Supreme Court to overturn the decision she precipitated in *Roe v. Wade,* she continues to contribute to pro-life activities.

Despite their success, it has become increasingly difficult for the pro-life side to maintain a presence at abortion facilities. Sidewalk counselors now find their work restricted by the passage of the Freedom of Access to Clinic Entrances Act and face arrest whenever they assemble to protest abortion at a facility. Recently, members of a Connecticut pro-life advocacy organization were arrested and incarcerated for "blocking a clinic entrance" because they were attempting to provide a prayerful presence outside a New Haven abortion facility. No entrance was blocked, but the police said that since the protesters were standing on the sidewalk, women had to "walk around them" to get into the clinic. Hoping to begin to challenge the legitimacy of the Freedom of Access to Clinic Entrances Act, the Connecticut counselors now face significant legal costs and lost wages due to a protracted schedule of court appearances.

While maintaining its sidewalk activism, the pro-life side continues to promote legislation that will strengthen its political position. Acknowledging the important role that ultrasound technology can play in helping change women's minds about abortion, Congressman Cliff Stearns (R-FL) introduced the Informed Choice Act (H.R. 216) in the House of Representatives early in 2005, with Senator Jim Bunning (R-KY) sponsoring the bill in the Senate. The Informed Choice Act would authorize the secretary of Health and Human Services to make grants to nonprofit tax-exempt organizations for the purchase of ultrasound equipment to provide free ultrasound exams to pregnant women desiring the service. Each pregnant woman upon whom the ultrasound equipment is used must be shown the visual image of the fetus from the ultrasound examination and given a general description of it. The examining physician must also give the woman the approximate age of her fetus. Finally, the woman must be given information on abortion, and alternatives to abortion such as childbirth and adoption, as well as information about agencies that will assist her in taking advantage of these alternatives.

The Informed Choice Act is one of those "political" initiatives that is actually nonpolitical.[23] The National Study of Women's Attitudes Toward Ultrasound Technology, completed in 2003, concluded that nearly nine in ten women (87 percent) said it is important for nonprofit women's health centers to provide ultrasound services. Four out of five women (81 percent) would urge their member of Congress to vote for legislation like the Informed Choice Act.[24]

The advent of high-quality ultrasound shows how developments outside the political sphere can affect the politics of abortion. A growing number of people in the pro-choice movement have realized that whether or not to have an abortion involves a complex moral calculus. Many women "choose" abortion because they truly believe there is no other choice. They are often desperate and it is simply not enough to show them an ultrasound image to convince them of the value of carrying their child to term. Often unsupported by partners, parents, or employers, these women may not be aware of the community services that are available.[25] Advocacy groups like Feminists for Life have focused on the unmet needs of women so that they are no longer pressured into the choice for abortion. While Feminists for Life have opposed the family-cap provision of welfare

CHAPTER TEN

Ending
the Abortion Wars

WHILE THERE HAVE been many casualties in the abortion wars, truth has been the first and most frequent casualty. The abortion battles escalated in the fall of 2005 when President George W. Bush nominated Judge John Roberts to the Supreme Court. Senator Barbara Boxer, a fierce opponent of Roberts, claimed during the hearings that if *Roe v. Wade* were overturned, "five thousand women a year will die." This statistic was invented by NARAL leaders more than three decades ago. Bernard Nathanson, a founder of the organization who eventually turned his back on abortion, says, "We spoke of 5,000–10,000 deaths a year—even though we knew the figures were totally false. But it was a useful figure—widely accepted and powerful, so why go out of our way to correct it with honest statistics?"[1]

Government data support Nathanson's recollections. The National Center for Health Statistics reveals that after penicillin became available to control infection, the number of deaths from illegal abortion averaged around 250 per year through the 1950s. By 1966, with abortion still illegal in all states, the number of deaths had dropped to 120 as a result of new and better antibiotics and the establishment of intensive-care units in hospitals. By the time of *Roe v. Wade* in 1973, the annual death rate for illegal abortion had fallen to just 24, rising to 26 in 1974, after abortion was legalized.[2]

Aside from the inaccuracy about the number of abortion deaths, comments such as Boxer's are also deceptive in their implication that overturning *Roe* would instantly criminalize abortion. A study by the Life Legal Defense Fund reported that "more than two-thirds of the states have repealed their abortion laws to conform to *Roe v. Wade* and *Doe v. Bolton,* which allow abortion for any reason before viability and for nearly any reason after viability." Even if *Roe* were overturned and the states were left to decide about the legality of abortion, only seven states—Louisiana, Michigan, Oklahoma, Rhode Island, South Dakota, Wisconsin, and Arkansas—would have enforceable laws on the books that would prohibit abortion.[3] In the other forty-three states and the District of Columbia, which account for more than 90 percent of the population, abortion would be legal for most or all reasons throughout pregnancy. Based on current abortion rates, the Life Legal Defense Fund estimates that even if *Roe* fell today, more than a million abortions per year would continue to be performed legally in the United States.

Ignoring these facts, the pro-choice Center for Reproductive Rights maintains that "in 30 states, women are at risk of losing their right to choose abortion after a reversal of *Roe,*" and that twenty-one of these states warrant "the highest level of concern." The Center warns, "Old laws are on the books that could ban abortion right away in many states. In states where the old laws have never been blocked by a court, state officials could begin enforcing these laws immediately."[4]

At this point, no one can make confident predictions about what would happen in each individual state if *Roe* were to fall. In fact, given the evolution that Supreme Court justices undergo on the Court, it is impossible to predict how President Bush's Supreme Court nominees might vote in a challenge to *Roe.* Yet this did not stop NARAL and other abortion-rights advocates from attempting to destroy both Judge Roberts and Judge Alito before they even began their confirmation hearings. A NARAL television commercial that was later withdrawn accused Roberts of supporting a convicted abortion-clinic bomber, and of holding an ideology that "leads him to excuse violence against other Americans." The attack ad included the image of a severely injured abortion provider in a wheelchair, and showed pictures of a bomb-damaged clinic in Birmingham, Alabama—conveying a subliminal message that Judge Roberts had contributed to this violence.

The nonpartisan watchdog organization FactCheck.org immediately disseminated information revealing that "the ad was false." Far from supporting clinic bombers or those who perpetrate violence, the truth is that when Roberts was counsel to President Reagan he drafted a memo calling clinic bombers "criminals" who should be "prosecuted to the full extent of the law."[5]

Distortions like NARAL's anti-Roberts ad are not surprising. In an effort to frighten a new generation into supporting abortion, the pro-choice side recently resurrected a multimillion-dollar ad campaign featuring the wire coat-hanger symbol from a bygone day. Once a frightening icon of the horrors of illegal abortion—whose real toll, as we have seen, is constantly exaggerated—that image is completely lost on a new generation of women. The leaders on the pro-choice side also blame the younger generation for "not appreciating" their hard-won right to abortion. The August 2005 issue of *Glamour* magazine reported on the "mysterious disappearance of young pro-choice women" and concluded that these "young women just don't know how good they have it."[6] In its charge of ingratitude among the young, *Glamour* captures the sentiments of the older generation of angry activists like Sarah Weddington, the pro-choice attorney who argued the *Roe v. Wade* case more than thirty years ago. Recently, Weddington published an article about an experience she had on an airplane with a young flight attendant. Weddington was wearing her "1970s-era button depicting a coat hanger with a red slash through it." To Weddington, it obviously remained a powerful symbol, but to the younger woman, it meant nothing at all. As Weddington recalled, the flight attendant kept staring at her. "She would circle around and she'd come back and she'd look at it again." Finally the curious young woman asked her, "What do you have against coat hangers?"[7] To Weddington, this was cultural and historical illiteracy of the worst sort. Yet in an odd way, the young woman was right: the symbol that meant so much to the attorney was obsolete and had always been inaccurate.

Until now, the pro-choice advocates have been successful in

defining the decision of abortion as simply an issue of health or of a woman's choice—a privacy issue. But as abortion has increasingly become a matter of urgent public policy, as opposed to an isolated choice, momentum in the political debate has swung almost imperceptibly to the pro-life side. State legislators are beginning to respond to their pro-life constituents. In California, a petition drive placed the Parents' Right to Know and Child Protection Initiative, which would require that abortion providers notify at least one parent of a minor girl before aborting her baby, on the ballot in 2005. Although the initiative lost by a slim margin, it showed that unrestricted abortion was losing ground in one of the most liberal states in the nation. And California, as all observers know, is a proving ground for political movements that later travel to the rest of the country. In March 2006—a few days after the Supreme Court ruled that the pro-choice side could no longer use RICO laws to halt protests at abortion clinics—Governor Mike Rounds signed into law a bill passed by the South Dakota legislature banning abortion except when the mother's life is in danger.

In addition to the growing number of pro-life initiatives at the state level, federal lawmakers have sponsored legislation designed to protect the unborn and the newborn. The Born-Alive Infants Protection Act was designed to ensure that every infant born alive, including any infant who survives an abortion procedure, is considered a person under federal law. Signed by President Bush in August 2002, this law bans the so-called "live-birth abortion" in which the baby is delivered and then left to die in a utility room. Notoriously practiced at Christ Hospital in Oak Lawn, Illinois, and elsewhere, the procedure was revealed by Jill Stanek, a nurse at the hospital who testified at the congressional hearings on the Born-Alive Act.[8]

The fetus is given "person" status in the recently passed Unborn Victims of Violence Act, which dictates harsh penalties for injuring or killing an unborn child during the commission of a crime. The Unborn Child Pain Awareness Act would require that women be advised of the full facts about fetal pain and also be given an opportunity to request anesthesia for the unborn child during the abortion. And, although there have been many failures, Congress continues to attempt to ban the form of late-term abortion that uses dilation and extraction procedures—or "partial-birth abortion."[9] The federal legislation on the grisly late-term procedure follows several statewide bans.

It appears to have been the highly publicized testimony of doctors who performed this type of late-term abortion that galvanized the attention of citizens who were unaware of the full province of the abortion regime. While the public had believed that the partial-birth abortion procedure was "rare," testimony from those performing the procedure made it clear that thousands of these abortions were done each year—nearly all of them for the convenience or desire of the mother rather than because a problem pregnancy threatened her health. Even the partial-birth abortion supporter Ron Fitzsimmons, formerly the executive director of the National Coalition of Abortion Providers, now admits that he had "lied through [his] teeth" when he said that this form of abortion was rare and used only on women whose lives were in danger or whose fetuses were damaged.[10]

In congressional testimony on partial-birth abortion, Dr. Mitchell Creinin described the procedure:[11]

> *Question:* If the fetus is close to 24 weeks and you are performing a surgical abortion, you would be concerned about delivering the fetus entirely intact because that might result in a live baby that may survive, correct?
>
> *Answer:* You said I was performing an abortion, so since the objective of an abortion is to not have a live fetus, then that would be correct.
>
> *Question:* In your opinion, if you were performing a surgical abortion at 23 or 24 weeks, and the cervix was so dilated that the head could pass through without compression, you would do whatever you needed to do in order to make sure that the live baby was not delivered, wouldn't you?
>
> *Answer:* Whatever I needed, meaning whatever surgical procedure I needed to do as part of the procedure? Yes. Then the answer is Yes.
>
> *Question:* And one step you would take to avoid delivery of a live baby would be to hold the head of the fetus on the internal side of the cervical os in order to collapse the skull, is that right? (This is after the rest of the body of the fetus is already delivered and resting outside the mother's body.)
>
> *Answer:* Yes, because the objective of my procedure is to perform an abortion.

Question: And that would ensure you did not deliver a live baby?
Answer: Correct.

Another late-term abortion provider, Dr. Marilynn Frederiksen, when asked about whether or not the fetus would experience pain during the procedure used in late-term dilation and extraction, flippantly responded, "I have never talked to a fetus about whether or not it experiences pain." Dr. Frederiksen described her own technique for doing the late-term vaginal delivery procedure: Instead of using scissors to cut into the base of the unborn child's skull in order to compress it, Frederiksen said, "I use my finger to disrupt the central nervous system, thereby the skull collapses and I can easily deliver the remainder of the fetus through the cervix." When asked whether she tells the mother she is going to "collapse the skull," Frederiksen said that she did not.[12]

Some doctors who testified told members of Congress that they tried to make the procedure less traumatic for the mothers by hiding some of the facts from them—especially information about the need for an incision at the base of the unborn child's skull to ensure the delivery of a dead fetus. Dr. Amos Grunebaum said that if a mother wants to see the fetus after the abortion, he will often attempt to conceal the incision at the base of the skull: "The fetus will be dressed like a newborn—it will be dressed and kind of have a little hat placed on it so only the face was visible."[13]

Despite a mainstream media that continues to refer to partial-birth abortion as "so-called partial-birth abortion," the majority of Americans are now becoming aware of the negative effects that abortion has had on women, and on their families. A 2005 Harris Interactive poll claims that 52 percent of Americans favor *Roe v. Wade* and 47 percent oppose it. (The poll erroneously describes *Roe* as the Supreme Court decision that made abortion legal through the third month of pregnancy. The reality is that *Roe*, in conjunction with the 1973 companion case, *Doe v. Bolton,* made abortion legal through all nine months of pregnancy.)[14] The same poll found that 72 percent of Americans said that abortion should be illegal in the second three months of pregnancy, and 86 percent said abortion should be illegal in the last three months of pregnancy.[15] Even support for abortion in the first three months is now open to debate.

In a 2004 Zogby International poll, 61 percent of Americans said abortion should not be permitted after the fetal heartbeat has begun.[16] This occurs in the first month.[17] A recent Wirthlin World-wide poll reported that 61 percent of respondents said abortion is "almost always bad" for women.[18]

The data demonstrate that women who have had abortions are six times more likely to commit suicide than women who have given birth. Induced abortion increases the risk of placenta separation in subsequent pregnancies by 50 percent and doubles the risk of preterm birth in later pregnancies. Epidemiological studies as well as breast physiology suggest a causal link between induced abortion and breast cancer, independent of the delay of a first full-term pregnancy.[19]

Feminists are no longer automatically pro-abortion. Erika Bachiochi, editor of *The Cost of "Choice,"* points out that the earliest feminists including Susan B. Anthony, Elizabeth Cady Stanton, and Mary Wollstonecraft, who fought so hard for women's rights, would have been appalled at the thought of celebrating abortion as a symbol of women's freedom and equality. Alice Paul, author of the original Equal Rights Amendment of 1923, called abortion "the ultimate exploitation of women."[20]

Young men—even young black rap artists who are unlikely conscripts for the pro-life movement—are also questioning abortion. A few years ago, in the mega-hit "One Mic," hip-hop artist NAS asked women to stop abortion because "we need more warriors here." More recently, rap star Nick Cannon's video for his song "Can I Live" tells the story of his own teenage mother's "choice" as she entered an abortion clinic with the intention of ending her pregnancy. While she sits in the waiting room, she is "visited" by the apparition of her would-be son (Nick), who pleads with her to "make the right decision, and don't go through with this knife decision." Dressed all in white, Cannon plays the unborn child as a singing "angel" giving voice to his desire to be born. Throughout the music video he tries to connect with his mother and to plead his case for the right to his own life. At one point he laments, "I don't like this clinic.... What you want, morning sickness or the sickness of mourning?" In the last scenes, Cannon's teenage mother rises from the operating table as her unborn son's arguments finally get through to her, and she runs from the clinic into the light of day. Outside, she is greeted by dozens of smiling young children singing the chorus—and all wearing T-shirts with the words "Can I Live" printed on them.[21]

Cannon responded to the interest in his video by posting the following message on the board at his official fan site:

> This record is extremely important to me and to our community. There are a lot of young mothers in need and who have had to struggle to raise their children. I just wanted to recognize all the strong women who are raising children on their own like my mother had to do. Myself and my foundation really want to help these women. If any of you out there know a single mother between the ages of 15–25 who may be having a difficult time, I would love to hear the story. Please write to me and explain the condition and how I could possibly help. I will check the website and respond.[22]

Some on the pro-choice side have complained that Cannon has become "the darling of the anti-abortion movement" because of his "simplistic message." Renee Graham, a *Boston Globe* columnist, warned that "the implications of 'Can I Live' reach far beyond chart position or airplay; it oversimplifies a very divisive and difficult issue. Cannon may claim he is just telling his story, but…it's less a thoughtful consideration of his mother's choice than one big guilt trip. Opting to be preachy and pedantic, he ignores that the ramification of choosing not to have an abortion can be just as profound and complex as the choice to have one."[23]

At one time, Graham's angry response to Cannon's video might have won the day, and pro-choice advocates, by applying pressure to radio stations and threatening boycotts of MTV and BET, would have succeeded in blocking the song from the air. But "Can I Live" was voted in the top ten at the music-video rating site for several weeks.

In response to the growing pro-life momentum, Senator Barbara Boxer again introduced new federal legislation in 2004 that would end any state efforts to regulate abortion and instead create federal laws to protect a woman's right to choose. The new version of the Freedom of Choice Act would "establish a statutory right to choose within the same parameters articulated by the Supreme Court in *Roe v. Wade*." With provisions protecting abortion that are even stronger than *Roe v. Wade,* this legislation would ensure that "a poor woman cannot be denied the use of Medicaid if she chooses to have an abortion; that abortions cannot be prohibited at public hospitals, giving women more choices than private clinics; and that women serving our country in the military overseas would be able to obtain safe abortions performed in a military hospital."[24] The legislation, which has so far gained no traction, looks backward to the glory days nearly four decades ago when a savvy marketing strategy, working with a powerful new feminist movement, was able to define abortion as a "choice" that would serve the well-being of the individual and the nation.

But today, abortion-rights groups like NARAL, NOW, and Planned Parenthood are not quite the power players they used to be. A recent *Wall Street Journal* article pointed out that political donations to the National Organization for Women shriveled from $327,000 in 1992 to $44,000 in 2004. Meanwhile, Planned Parenthood Federation of America, Inc., facing a revolt among affiliates because of the group's politicization, recently ousted its president and never took a position on the Roberts nomination. And the new president at NARAL Pro-Choice America was forced to fire its director of media communications as a result of the backlash over the dishonest anti-Roberts attack ads. Looking at such developments, the *Wall Street Journal* summarized the pro-choice movement as precarious: "Internal squabbles, declining membership and complacency during the Clinton years have left most women's rights groups in weakened shape."[25]

By the beginning of Samuel Alito's Supreme Court confirmation hearings in early 2006, the pro-choice movement had an opportunity to reassert its power by attacking the jurist whose views on abortion seemed less ambiguous than those of Judge Roberts. There were attack ads warning of the "extremist" conservative nominee by the People for the American Way and MoveOn.org, and dire predictions in the *New York Times* that Alito "might join Justices Scalia and Thomas in supporting conservative activism." But neither NOW nor NARAL seemed able to gather the strength to mount a real attack.[26] Opting instead to enlist a handful of liberal senators in the Democratic Party to fight their battle against Alito, the aging feminists were noticeably silent throughout the confirmation process. But lawmakers such as Ted Kennedy, Pat Leahy, Joe Biden, and Charles Schumer seemed to substitute posturing and lectures for incisive questioning. At the end of the first day of the Alito hearings, staffers released an analysis of how much time each senator had spent talking during his chance to question the candidate. Each senator was given 30 minutes for questions, but Leahy spent more than 18 minutes talking and Kennedy took up 24 minutes of his 30-minute allotment lecturing to the audience rather than asking questions. Senator Biden likewise talked so long that only 6 minutes of his allotted time remained for Judge Alito to respond.[27]

While it should not have been surprising that the senators spent most of their time expressing their own opinions on issues rather than finding out the opinions of the nominee, it was surprising that so little attention was focused on abortion throughout the hearings. While Newsday.com reported that "abortion figured in 101 out of 546 questions posed to Alito," it never developed into the issue, as had been predicted, that would transform the hearings into an epic social battle.[28] Abortion was the dog that did not bark.

It is difficult to know whether this silence arose from an awareness by those questioning Alito that most people have already grown weary of contentious talk about abortion—or if the senators were only going through the motions in a halfhearted attempt to give the pro-choice advocates just enough pro-choice rhetoric to keep the constituency satisfied. Whatever the reason, the Alito hearings suggest that the country may simply be tired of the battle over abortion. To begin to build upon this emerging weariness, the pro-life side would do well to move away from the contentious philosophical and personal confrontations of the past, and begin real conversations with the other side.

In *Abortion Rites*, Marvin Olasky, a journalism professor at the University of Texas, argues that the pro-life side should begin to capitalize on this culture change by exerting "steady pressure through all the means that worked a century ago to reduce abortion and are beginning to work anew: education about abstinence, refuges for the abandoned, provision of adoption and many other services." From the earliest days of abortion in America, the first pro-life organizations were service groups that provided direct aid and adoption assistance to women.[29] While his book on the history of abortion and abortion law in America acknowledges that overturning permissive abortion laws and passing protections for the unborn are important goals, Olasky suggests that it is even more important to begin to change a culture that makes abortion a "solution" to a problem: "A pro-life activist who believes a change of law will eliminate abortion ignores the late nineteenth century lesson that law by itself avails little unless programs emphasizing prevention and offering true compassion are in place and effective."[30] Some pro-life leaders like to equate their movement with that of the abolitionists, but Olasky maintains that they have chosen the wrong heroes: "Men such as William Lloyd Garrison and John Brown precipitated a tragic civil war in which six hundred thousand died and the enslaved objects of their compassion ended up leaving the Scylla of slavery only to fall prey to the Charybdis of sharecropping, lynching, and the Ku Klux Klan."[31]

Rather than continuing to fight an angry and sometimes violent war on abortion, the "better model" for the pro-life movement now, says Olasky, would be the containment policy that the United States successfully applied toward the Soviet Union from the late 1940s through 1991. For this reason, Olasky advises that "the pro-life movement today needs Eisenhowers, not John Browns. It needs leaders who understand that in America there has always been some abortion among women seduced by men, money or the religion of self. That is sad, but the tragedy becomes gargantuan only when those three groups expand to become part of an evil empire and when those on the outskirts of the groups come to consider abortion the norm."[32] In this view, the pro-life goal should be to help Americans view abortion as a non-normative practice that is unworthy of societal approval.

If abortion is to be contained, the provision of compassionate alternatives going beyond graphic posters and angry words is of key importance. That these compassionate alternatives are already in place was recently acknowledged by the *New York Times,* whose editorial policy has been unwavering for decades. In a sympathetic report on the growing number of crisis pregnancy centers and post-abortion recovery groups, John Leland writes: "In their quiet way, they represent a dimension of the anti-abortion movement that is just as passionate and far-reaching, consisting not of protesters or political activists but of Christian therapy groups, crisis pregnancy centers, adoption ministries, and support programs for single mothers and their children." Leland estimates that the number of crisis pregnancy centers ranges from 2,300 to 3,500 nationwide, compared with about 1,800 abortion providers. Traveling to Louisville, Kentucky, to interview some of the beneficiaries of these services, he spent several days at A Woman's Choice, an offshoot of the largest church in Kentucky, and reported: "Over a two day period at the center, the message to women was consistent: abortion was psychologically and physically damaging, and that God would help provide for their children, however difficult the women's straits, and in the short term, the center would supply some necessities."[33]

Our cultural and political experience following *Roe* has shown that laws imposed from the top down create chaos and dissension. The sociologist James Davison Hunter suggests that the best way to resolve the conflicts provoked by *Roe* is through local and regional debate—among people who live and work in relative proximity to each other and who care about their common neighborhoods and communities, towns and cities, and regions; and within institutions that are prominent and integrated into the communities where these people live. "As Tocqueville observed on his trip to America," Hunter writes, "democracy flourishes in small-scale (that is, decentralized or local) settings. In such settings, local institutions and elites can play a genuinely mediating role, for there is, by the very circumstances of the collective life, accountability to each other and to others."[34]

Some of these conversations have already begun. During the debates over federal funding for pregnant women, people on the pro-life and pro-choice sides worked together to try to defeat the family caps. Both sides decried the unwillingness of the federal government to support pregnant women receiving welfare. Neither side wants women to need abortions because they do not have the money to raise a child. Most recently, groups such as Feminists for Life and Focus on the Family have joined Planned Parenthood to promote the Elizabeth Cady Stanton Pregnant and Parenting Student Services Act of 2005. The act, inspired by Feminists for Life's College Outreach Program, was introduced in both the Senate and the House of Representatives in November 2005. If passed, it would create a program to provide $10 million for two hundred grants to encourage colleges and universities to establish offices serving pregnant and parenting students.[35]

A few years ago, *Marie Claire* magazine provided a "changing places" opportunity for each side in the abortion debate. The magazine convinced the director of Life Perspectives, a pro-life feminist organization based in San Diego, to spend a day shadowing the director of the Hope Clinic for Women in Illinois, a provider of first- and second-trimester abortions. A few weeks later, the abortion-clinic director was invited to spend a day at the Life Perspectives offices. Interviews with each of the women following the "changing places" experience revealed that although both were offended by some of the activities of the other, each agreed that discussions must continue because meeting women's needs was a common aim. These cooperative ventures offer the greatest hope for the future. As James Hunter writes, "The people most receptive to the idea of talking and even working together to resolve differences are those who deal with women facing unplanned pregnancies on a day-to-day basis, either those who run abortion clinics or homes for pregnant women."[36]

Living in a democracy and dealing with an issue such as abortion that divides the country in half demands that we recover the language of public argument, and move beyond the superficial slogans that rally the troops but build impenetrable barriers. Taking the discussions out of the courts and back to the realm of local policy, where we might once again debate the politics of abortion as neighbors and friends, would be a good start.

ACKNOWLEDGMENTS

I AM INDEBTED to the members of the Advisory Council of the James Madison Program in American Ideals and Institutions at Princeton University, and especially to the director of the Madison Program, Robert P. George, for the support they provided during my tenure as a visiting fellow. The opportunity to spend a year at Princeton—participating in seminars, attending lectures, teaching, and learning from some of the smartest people in the nation—was wonderful. I will always be grateful.

I am also thankful for the support I have received from the University of San Diego. In particular, I am grateful to Patrick Drinan, dean of the College of Arts and Sciences, who made my year at Princeton possible, and to Rosemary Getty of the University of San Diego Law School, whose tireless devotion to the fostering of research and writing is greatly appreciated.

I am grateful for my Connecticut family—as well as my "extended" Connecticut family, including Bette Jayne and Hugh St. Leger of Connecticut Right to Life. I have been inspired by the courage of Fr. John Bevins, pastor of the Church of the Immaculate Conception, and Fr. Joseph Looney of St. Margaret's Church in Waterbury, Connecticut. Thank you also to Ann Scheidler for her willingness to spend hours talking with me about her family's twenty-year court battle with the National Organization for Women—including three trips to the Supreme Court. I am grateful to Ann for her willingness to share all the details.

Finally, thank you to Encounter's Peter Collier once again for being a skillful and encouraging editor, and to Carol Staswick for her incomparable attention to detail.

And, of course, a special thank you to Dana, Heidi, and Jonathan—for everything.

NOTES

INTRODUCTION

1 James Davison Hunter, *Before the Shooting Begins: Searching for Democracy in America's Culture Wars* (New York: Free Press, 1994), p. 18.
2 Sally Blackmun, Introduction to Gloria Feldt, *The War on Choice* (New York: Random House, 2004), p. xix.
3 Ibid.
4 Bernard H. Siegan, *The Supreme Court's Constitution: An Inquiry into Judicial Review and Its Impact on Society* (New Brunswick, New Jersey: Transaction, 1993), p. 149.
5 Mary Anne Glendon, *Abortion and Divorce in Western Law* (Cambridge, Massachusetts: Harvard University Press, 1987).
6 Bernard Nathanson, *The Hand of God: A Journey from Death to Life by the Abortion Doctor Who Changed His Mind* (Washington, D.C.: Regnery, 1996).
7 Gertrude Himmelfarb, *One Nation, Two Cultures* (New York: Alfred A. Knopf, 1999), p. 116.
8 Nathanson, *The Hand of God.*
9 Hunter, *Before the Shooting Begins,* p. 4.
10 Ibid., p. 174.
11 Kristin Luker, *Abortion and the Politics of Motherhood* (Berkeley: University of California Press, 1985).

CHAPTER 1: LOOKING FOR THE LIFE OF THE PARTY

1 In *Theological Ethics, Moral Philosophy, and Public Moral Discourse,* cited in Paul Likoudis, "Who Should Be Denied Communion?" *Wanderer,* May 13, 2004.
2 Cited in Likoudis, "Who Should Be Denied Communion?"
3 Bernard Nathanson, *The Hand of God: A Journey from Death to Life by the Abortion Doctor Who Changed His Mind* (Washington, D.C.: Regnery, 1996), p. 86.
4 Ibid., p. 88.
5 Ibid., p. 89.
6 Emily Ullman, The 2002 Profile in Courage Award Essay, John F. Kennedy Library Foundation.
7 Sen. Edward M. Kennedy, letter to Mr. Thomas E. Dennelly, August 3, 1971, published in Catholic League for Religious and Civil Rights news release, August 3, 2005, www.catholicleague.org/05press_releases/quarter%203/050803_KennedyLetter.htm
8 Cited by Vasu Murti, "The Liberal Case against Abortion," www.all-creatures.org
9 Mary Meehan, "Abortion: The Left Has Betrayed the Sanctity of Life," *Progressive,* September 1980, pp. 61–62.
10 Both cited by Murti, "The Liberal Case against Abortion."
11 Jay G. Sykes, "Farewell to Liberalism," *Insight* (Sunday magazine of the *Milwaukee Journal*), September 8, 1974, pp. 30–32.
12 ACLU Executive Committee, minutes of July 30, 1977 meeting, ACLU Archives, Box 117, folder 1. For other examples of dissent within the ranks of the ACLU, see the ACLU publication, *Civil Liberties,* April 1970; November 6, 1974; Winter 1986; Spring 1986; Summer/Fall 1986. See also, Nat Hentoff, "A Heretic in the ACLU," *Washington Post,* August 16, 1985, p. A23; cited in Mary Meehan, "ACLU v. Unborn Children," *Human Life Review,* Spring 2001.
13 Rosemary Bottcher, "Pro-Abortionists Poison Feminism," in *Pro-Life Feminism: Different Voices* (Toronto: Life Cycle Books, 1985), p. 45.
14 Ibid.
15 Cited by Murti, "The Liberal Case against Abortion."
16 "A Mouse That Roars Turns 25: An Interview with CFFC President Frances Kissling," May 1998, www.catholicsforchoice.org/aboutus2.htm
17 Ibid.
18 Cited by Murti, "The Liberal Case against Abortion."
19 Nat Hentoff, "Life of the Party," *New Republic,* June 19, 2000.
20 William Clinton, *My Life* (New York: Knopf, 2004), p. 229.
21 Hentoff, "Life of the Party."
22 Ibid.

23 John Leo, "Here Come the Wild Creatures," *U.S. News & World Report,* October 19, 1992.

24 Murti, "The Liberal Case against Abortion."

25 "Robert P. Casey, Former Pennsylvania Governor, Dies at 68," CNN.com, May 31, 2000, www.cnn.com/2000/allpolitics/ stories/05/30/bc.obit.casey.ap/index.htm

26 *Boston Globe,* January 30, 2000, p. A30, www.issues2000.org

27 On the Issues: Al Gore on Abortion, www.issues2000.org

28 Bill Turque, *Inventing Al Gore* (Boston: Mariner Books, 2000).

29 Democrat Party debate in Los Angeles, March 1, 2000, www.issues2000.org

30 Cited by David Enrich, "Kucinich's Choice," *National Review Online,* February 20, 2003, www.nationalreview.com

31 On the Issues: Dennis Kucinich on the issues, www.issues.2000.org/ Dennis_Kucinich.htm

32 Enrich, "Kucinich's Choice."

33 Jonathan V. Last, "Wesley Clark Takes a Stand on Abortion," *Weekly Standard,* January 22, 2004.

34 Ibid.

35 Religious Freedom Coalition, January 17, 2004, www.rfcnet.org

36 Al Sharpton, *Al on America* (New York: Dafina Books, 2002), p. 89.

37 Peter Kirsanow, "Abortion Absolutism," *National Review Online,* June 15, 2004, www.nationalreview.com

38 Cited in ibid.

39 Ibid.

40 Ibid.

41 Ibid.

42 "Poll–The Democratic Delegates," posted on the website of Democrats for Life, www.democratsforlife.org

43 Mark Shields, "The Tolerant Democrats," CNN.com, July 21, 2003.

44 Paul Greenberg, "Democrats for Life?" *Washington Times,* February 24, 2005.

45 David Kirkpatrick, "For Democrats, Rethinking Abortion Runs Risks," *New York Times,* February 16, 2005.

46 Ibid.

47 Ibid.

48 Ibid.

49 Kimberly Schuld, *Guide to Feminist Organizations* (Washington, D.C.: Capital Research Center, 2002), p. 189.

50 Ibid.

51 Data compiled by Cleta Mitchell, Esq., Foley & Lardner, Washington, D.C.

52 Peggy Noonan, "A Tough Roe," *OpinionJournal,* from the *Wall Street Journal* editorial page, January 20, 2003, www.opinionjournal.com

53 Zogby International, "New National Abortion Poll Shows Majority of Americans Are Pro-Life," January 16, 2004, www.zogby.com/ soundbites/readclips.dbm?ID=6982

CHAPTER 2: RACE AND THE POLITICS OF ABORTION

1   Allan R. Andrews, "Opinion Voiced as a Cartoon," *Pacific Stars and Stripes*, Tokyo, April 17, 1997.
2   Anthony Bradley, "Abortion by Race," *WORLD*, February 19, 2005.
3   Bob McPhail, "How Many Abortions in California: The State Doesn't Want You to Know," *San Diego News Notes*, May 2002, www.sdnewsnotes.com/ed/articles/2002/0502bm.htm
4   Gregg Cunningham, "Why Abortion Is Genocide," Center for Bio-Ethical Reform, www.abortionNO.org
5   Reverend Johnny Hunter, "Abortion: The Robbing of a Heritage," www.pregnantpause.org/racism/robherit.htm
6   Bradley, "Abortion by Race."
7   Ibid.
8   Michael W. Perry, *The Pivot of Civilization in Historical Perspective* (Seattle: Inkling Books, 2001).
9   Stephen Mosher, "The Repackaging of Margaret Sanger," *Wall Street Journal*, May 5, 1997.
10 Ibid.
11 Margaret Sanger, *The Pivot of Civilization*, with introduction by H. G. Wells and foreword by Peter C. Engelman (1922; Amherst, New York: Humanity Books, 2003), p. 131.
12 Ibid., p. 133.
13 Mosher, "The Repackaging of Margaret Sanger."
14 Perry, *The Pivot of Civilization in Historical Perspective*, p. 17.
15 Mosher, "The Repackaging of Margaret Sanger."
16 Robert W. Brown, "Provider Availability, Race and Abortion Demand," *Southern Economic Journal*, January 1, 2001.
17 Ibid.
18 "Little Notes," *San Diego News Notes*, February 2003.
19 Ibid.
20 Jennifer Jacobson, "A Sense of Purpose Shaped by Faith and Trauma," *Chronicle of Higher Education*, May 7, 2004.
21 Book jacket notes for Sanger, *The Pivot of Civilization*, 2003 edition.
22 John J. Donohue and Steven D. Levitt, "The Impact of Legalized Abortion on Crime," U.C. Berkeley Law and Economics Working Paper Series, No. 2000-18, downloaded from the Social Science Research Network Electronic Paper Collection at http://papers. ssrn.com/
23 Ibid., p. 14.
24 Ibid., p. 34.

25 Ramesh Ponnuru, "Abortion Is Not the Answer to Crime," *Wall Street Journal,* August 22, 1999.

26 Steven D. Levitt and Stephen J. Dubner, *Freakonomics* (New York: HarperCollins, 2005), p. 141.

CHAPTER 3: *INSIDE ABORTION INSIDE WASHINGTON*

1 William Saletan, *Bearing Right: How Conservatives Won the Abortion War* (Berkeley: University of California Press, 2003), p. 218.

2 Dorothy Roberts, *Killing the Black Body* (New York: Vintage Books, 1997), p. 233.

3 Cited by Saletan, *Bearing Right*, p. 218.

4 Ibid., p. 220.

5 Ibid., p. 221.

6 Ibid.

7 Cited by Fr. Frank Pavone, "Uniting for Life," *Priests for Life Newsletter,* Winter 1994.

8 Ibid.

9 Ibid.

10 Ibid.

11 Cited by Saletan, *Bearing Right*, p. 229.

12 Public Law 104-193, section 401 (a).

13 The Alan Guttmacher Institute, "Welfare Reform, Marriage and Sexual Behavior," www.agi-usa.org/pubs/ib_welfare_reform.html

14 Ibid.

15 Ted Goertzel, "Defending New Jersey's Family Cap Welfare Reform in the Courts," paper prepared for the Eastern Sociological Society Meetings, Baltimore, Maryland, March 4, 2000, available at http://crab.rutgers.edu/~defendingthecap.doc

16 Christopher H. Smith, "Family Cap Causing Abortions," Address to the House of Representatives, *Congressional Record,* June 16, 1998.

17 Goertzel, "Defending New Jersey's Family Cap Welfare Reform in the Courts."

18 Ibid.

19 Ibid.

20 Saletan, *Bearing Right*, p. 233.

21 "Biography of a Bad Statistic," Annenberg Political Fact Check, May 25, 2005, www.factcheck.org

22 Ibid.

23 "Howard Dean's Abortion Myth," editorial, *Washington Times,* June 9, 2005.

24 Lawrence B. Finer and Stanley K. Henshaw, "Estimates of U.S. Abortion Incidence in 2001 and 2002," The Alan Guttmacher Institute, May 18, 2005.

25 Ibid.

26 Randy O'Bannon and Laura Hussey, "Claims That President Bush's Policies Increased Abortion Numbers Baseless," *LifeNews.com,* October 20, 2004, www.lifenews.com/nat886b.html

27 Glen Harold Stassen and Gary Krane, "Why Abortion Rate Is Up in Bush Years," *Houston Chronicle,* October 17, 2004.

28 Ibid.

29 O'Bannon and Hussey, "Claims That President Bush's Policies Increased Abortion Numbers Baseless."

CHAPTER 4: THE PERSONAL IS POLITICAL

1 G. Davidson Smith, "Single Issue Terrorism," *Commentary No. 74,* Canadian Security Intelligence Service publication, January 11, 2000, www.csis-scrs.gc.ca/eng/comment/com74_e.html

2 James Risen and Judy Thomas, "Pro-Life Turns Deadly: The Impact of Violence on America's Anti-Abortion Movement," *Newsweek,* January 26, 1998.

3 Kara Lowentheil, "First Assassination of Abortion Provider: 12 Years Ago This Month," *Choice Magazine* (Planned Parenthood), March 15, 2005.

4 Ibid.

5 "Justifiable Homicide: The Signers," Southern Poverty Law Center Intelligence Report, Summer 1998.

6 "Who Is Shelley Shannon? Shelley Is a Soldier," www.armyofgod. com/shelleywhois.html

7 Ibid.

8 Ibid.

9 Paul Hill, "Defending the Defenseless," in *The Abortion Controversy,* Current Controversies Series (San Diego: Greenhaven Press, 2001).

10 Army of God website, www.armyofgod.com

11 Ibid., www.armyofgod.com/JohnSalviIII.html

12 Ibid.

13 National Abortion Federation report, "Incidents of Violence and Disruption against Abortion Providers," 2004.

14 "Eric Robert Rudolph," *Wikipedia,* http://en.widipedia.org/wiki/Eric_Robert_Rudolph

15 Eric Robert Rudolph statement at sentencing, www.cnn.com/2005/LAW/04/13/rudolph.statement.ap/index.htm

16 Anti-Defamation League, "Extremist Chatter Praises Eric Rudolph As Hero," June 3, 2002, www.adl.org/NR/exeres/F429BE24-7477-4B79-8250-5F34627D43F3,0B1523CA-D

17 Joseph M. Scheidler, *CLOSED: 99 Ways to Stop Abortion* (Rockford, Illinois: Tan Books, 1985), p. 300.

18 "*NOW v. Scheidler* Timeline: The Complete Story," *National NOW*

Times (National Organization for Women), Fall 2002, www.now. org/nnt/fall-2002/timeline.html

19 Michelle Martin, "The Supreme Test," *Catholic New World,* December 8, 2002, www.catholicnewworld.com/archive/cnw2002/ 120802/supreme_120802.html

20 "*NOW v. Scheidler* Timeline: The Complete Story."

21 Ibid.

22 Ibid.

23 Stephen Vincent, "Scheidler's Supreme Victory," www.orthodoxytoday.org, 2003.

24 Robyn Blumner, "RICO: Be Careful What You Wish For," *Human Life Review,* June 22, 1998.

25 Jonathan Turley, *Charlotte Observer,* December 4, 2002.

26 Martin, "The Supreme Test."

27 Supreme Court of the United States, *NOW v. Scheidler,* December 4, 2002.

28 Pro-Life Action News, "U.S. Supreme Court Hears Scheidler Appeal," *Action News,* vol. 21, no. 3 (December 2002), www.prolifeaction.org/news/200212/ussc_nopix.html

29 "Supreme Court Hears *NOW v. Scheidler,*" National Organization for Women, December 4, 2002, www.now.org/press/12-02/ 12-04.html?printable

30 Pro-Life Action League, www.prolifeaction.org/index.php

31 Personal communication with Ann Scheidler, November 2005.

32 David Stout, "Supreme Court Backs Abortion Protesters in Unanimous Ruling," *New York Times,* February 28, 2006.

33 Ibid.

34 Ibid.

35 Kim Gandy, "Supreme Court Ends Protection against Abortion Clinic Violence," National Organization for Women website, February 28, 2006, www.now.org/press/02-06/02-28.html

36 Ibid.

37 Ibid.

38 Ann and Eric Scheidler, "Scheidler Wins Again in High Court," *Pro-Life Action News,* Winter 2006, www.prolifeaction.org/news/ 2006v25nl/scotus.htm

CHAPTER 5: THE POLITICS OF CELEBRATION

1 Refuse and Resist website, www.refuseandresist.org/ab/march10/ 2003/organizers.html

2 Daniel C. Maguire, *Sacred Choices: The Right to Contraception and Abortion in Ten World Religions* (Minneapolis: Fortress Press, 2001).

3 Joel Mowbray, "A Holiday for Abortion?" *FrontPage Magazine,*

March 10, 2004, www.frontpagemag.com/articles/printable. asp?ID=12536

4 Refuse and Resist initiated the National Day of Appreciation. Cosponsors include: Abortion Access Project, Abortion Clinics Online, ACLU Reproductive Freedom Project, American Medical Women's Association, Association of Reproductive Health Professionals, Boston Women's Health Book Collective, Catholics for a Free Choice, Center for Reproductive Rights, Choice USA, Feminist Majority Foundation, Medical Students for Choice, *Ms. Magazine,* NARAL Pro-Choice America, National Council of Jewish Women, National Network of Abortion Funds, National Organization for Women, Physicians for Reproductive Choice, Religious Coalition for Reproductive Choice, Third Wave. In cooperation with: National Abortion Federation, National Coalition of Abortion Providers, Planned Parenthood Federation of America. Endorsed by: June Barrett, David Gunn Jr., Emily Lyons, Gloria Steinem.

5 Refuse and Resist website, www.refuseandresist.org/ab/stop.antis. html

6 Refuse and Resist website, www.refuseandresist.org/ab/ 062897father.html

7 The Store, Planned Parenthood Federation of America, Inc., http://store.yahoo.com/ppfastore/ihadabt.html

8 Jennifer Baumgardner, "We're Not Sorry, Charlie," *Nation,* February 2, 2004.

9 Ibid.

10 Katha Pollitt, "In the Waiting Room," *Nation,* April 21, 2003.

11 *WorldNet Daily,* January 24, 2004, www.worldnetdaily.com

12 Rod Dreher, "Celebrating Roe," *National Review Online,* January 20, 2003, www.nationalreview.com

13 Ibid.

14 *Faith and Choices,* newsletter of the Religious Coalition for Reproductive Choice, Fall/Winter 2004.

CHAPTER 6: SACRED CHOICES

1 Cited by Michael J. Gorman and Ann Loar Brooks, *Holy Abortion?* (Eugene, Oregon: Wipf & Stock Publishers, 2004).

2 Katherine Hancock Ragsdale, "Sermons and Prayers," Religious Coalition for Reproductive Choice, www.rcrc.org/resources/ sermons_prayers/ragsdale_march_remarks.htm

3 Reverend Carlton Veazey, remarks at the March for Women's Lives, 2004, published in *Faith and Choices,* newsletter of the Religious Coalition for Reproductive Choice, Fall/Winter 2004.

4 Cited by Gorman and Brooks, *Holy Abortion?*

5 Ibid.

6 *Faith and Choices,* Fall/Winter 2004.

7 Ibid.

8 Ibid.

9 Ibid.

10 *Prayerfully Pro-Choice,* publication of the Religious Coalition for Reproductive Choice, pp. 73–74.

11 Cited by Gorman and Brooks, *Holy Abortion?*

12 Cited in ibid.

13 Cited in ibid.

14 *Prayerfully Pro-Choice,* pp. 85–86.

15 Daniel C. Maguire, *Sacred Choices: The Right to Contraception and Abortion in Ten World Religions* (Minneapolis: Fortress Press, 2001), p. viii.

16 Ibid., p. 27.

17 Ibid., p. 31.

18 Ibid., p. 34.

19 Ibid., p. 35.

20 Ibid., p. 37.

21 The Saint Antoninus Institute, *Pro-Life Shopping Guide* (Washington, D.C.: St. Antoninus Institute Press, 2001), p. 153.

22 Maguire, *Sacred Choices,* p. 119.

23 Ibid., p. 117.

24 Ibid., p. 101.

25 Ibid., p. 103.

26 Ibid., p. 105.

CHAPTER 7: CATHOLICS AND THE POLITICS OF ABORTION

1 Catechism of the Catholic Church, #2270, www.beliefnet.com/story/63/story-6328.html

2 Daniel A. Dombrowski and Robert Deltete, *A Brief, Liberal, Catholic Defense of Abortion* (Urbana, Illinois: University of Illinois Press, 2000), p. 24.

3 Ibid., p. 15.

4 Ibid., p. 24.

5 Anthony Padovano, review of *A Brief, Liberal, Catholic Defense of Abortion,* in *Conscience,* Summer 2000, www.catholicsforchoice.org/conscience/archived/dissentingview.htm

6 Kathryn Jean Lopez, "Aborting the Church: Frances Kissling and Catholics for a Free Choice," *Crisis,* April 1, 2002, www.crisismagazine.com/april2002/feature1.htm

7 Cited in ibid.

8 Cited in ibid.

9 Cited in ibid.

10 Catholics for a Free Choice, *Questions on Where Does Life Begin?* www.catholicsforchoice.org

11 Catholics for a Free Choice, *You Are Not Alone: Information for Young Catholic Women about the Abortion Decision,* www.catholicsforchoice.org/topics/abortion/documents/ 2000youarenotalone_000.pdf

12 Cited by Rosemary Ruether, "Catholics and Abortion: Authority vs. Dissent," *Christian Century,* October 3, 1985, pp. 859–62.

13 Kenneth Woodward, "Feminism and the Church," *Newsweek,* February 13, 1989, p. 60.

14 Michael Reilly, "'Free Choice' Catholics Issue Abortion Prayer Card," *NewsMax.com,* May 9, 2005, www.newsmax.com/archives/ articles/2005/5/8/224749.shtml

15 Cited by Lopez, "Aborting the Church."

16 Frances Kissling and Jon O'Brien, "Is God a Republican?" *Conscience,* Spring 2000, www.catholicsforchoice.org

17 Cited by Lopez, "Aborting the Church."

18 Kissling and O'Brien, "Is God a Republican?"

19 Brian Clowes, *Catholics for a Free Choice Exposed* (Font Royal, Virginia: Human Life International, 2001), p. 190.

20 Information on funding is from ibid., p. 51.

21 Alan Guttmacher Institute, 1995, cited by www.beliefnet.com/ story/63/story-6301-1.html

22 Alphonse deValk, "Politics, Abortion, and the Church, Part II," *Catholic Insight,* July 1, 2004.

23 Alphonse deValk, "John Kerry, the American Election, and Catholic Bishops," *Catholic Insight,* June 1, 2004.

24 "St. Louis Archbishop Warns of Upcoming Persecution over Abortion and Homosexuality," *LifeSite,* February 9, 2005, www.lifesitenews.com

25 DeValk, "John Kerry, the American Election, and Catholic Bishops."

26 Ibid.

27 Most Reverend Michael J. Sheridan, Bishop of Colorado Springs, Colorado, "On the Duties of Catholic Politicians and Voters," Pastoral Letter to the Catholic Faithful of the Diocese of Colorado Springs, May 1, 2004.

28 "Church Warned over Denying Communion," *Waterbury Republican American,* May 21, 2004, p. 7A.

29 Rosa DeLauro, "Catholic Democrats Release Statement of Principals," www.democrats.org/a/p/catholic_democrats_release_ statement_of_principals.html

30 "Catholic Politicians Seek a Pass from Bishops on Abortion," *Southern Cross,* March 9, 2006.

31 "Catholic Democrats Scolded on Abortion," *Washington Post,* March 11, 2006, p. A7.

32 Associated Press, "House Catholics Urged to Obey Moral Teaching," *Contra Costa Times,* March 16, 2006.

33 "Catholic Democrats Scolded on Abortion."

CHAPTER 8: CAMPUS POLITICS OF ABORTION

1 Tamar Lewin, "Catholics Adopt More Liberal Attitudes during College," *New York Times,* March 5, 2003.

2 Terry Vanderheyden and John Henry Westen, "Second Major Study Shows Modern Catholic Universities Harm Students' Faith Life," *LifeSite,* December 8, 2005, www.lifesitenews.com

3 Patrick J. Reilly, "The Enemy Inside the Gates: The Surrender of Catholic Higher Education," *Catholic Culture,* June 2004, www.catholicculture.org/docs/doc_view.cfm?recnum=6053

4 "Seven More Catholic Universities Found Promoting Planned Parenthood," *LifeSite,* December 9, 2002, www.lifesite.net

5 Erin R. Butcher and Patrick J. Reilly, *The Culture of Death on Catholic Campuses: A Five Year Review* (The Cardinal Newman Society, April 2004), p. 47.

6 Vanderheyden and Westen, "Second Major Study Shows Modern Catholic Universities Harm Students' Faith Life."

7 "New York Archdiocese Says Marist College 'No Longer Catholic,'" *Catholic Culture,* May 13, 2003, www.catholicculture.org/docs/doc_view.cfm?recnum=4674

8 Butcher and Reilly, *The Culture of Death on Catholic Campuses.*

9 Burton Bollag, "Who Is Catholic?" *Chronicle of Higher Education,* April 9, 2004.

10 Ashley Pavlic, "Casting Our Votes in Line with Science and Justice," *Daily Princetonian,* September 24, 2004.

11 "Human Rights for All," advertisement published in *Daily Princetonian,* October 19, 2004.

12 MIT Pro-Life, "Human Rights for All," www.MIT.edu/pro life/

13 Dartmouth Coalition for Life, www.dartmouth.edu/%7edcl/

14 Raymond L. Yu, "Student Views Clash in Abortion Debate," *Harvard Crimson,* March 4, 2005.

15 The American Collegians for Life, Student Leadership Conference, January 22–23, 2005, www.aclife.org/conference/schedule.html

16 Brian C. Anderson, "On Campus Conservatives Talk Back," *City Journal,* Winter 2005.

17 "Dissent vs. Vandalism," *Inside Higher Ed,* April 19, 2006, www.insidehighered.com/news/2006/04/19/nku

18 Brett Amelkian and Sophia Ahern Dwosh, "Vandals Tear Down Pro-Life Flag Display," *Daily Princetonian,* April 24, 2006,

www.dailyprincetonian.com/archives/2006/04/21/news/15337. shtml

19 John Henry Westen, "Pro-Life Display Destroyed at Washington University—Vandal Arrested," *LifeSite,* www.lifesite.net/ldn/2006/ may/06050309.html

CHAPTER 9: SIGNS OF LIFE

1 Matthew Nisbet, "They Bring Good Spin to Life: General Televised Promotion of the Pro-Life Agenda," *American Prospect Online,* June 14, 2002, www.prospect.org/webfeatures/2002/06/nisbet-m-06-14.html

2 Robert P. George and Christopher Wolfe, *Natural Law and Public Reason* (Washington, D.C.: Georgetown University Press, 2000), pp. 59–60.

3 Peter Singer, *Writings on an Ethical Life* (New York: Ecco Press, 2000), p. 160.

4 Ibid., p. 163.

5 Marvin Olasky, "Blue-State Philosopher," *WORLD,* November 27, 2004.

6 Robert P. George, *The Clash of Orthodoxies* (Wilmington, Delaware: ISI Books, 2001), p. 29.

7 General Electric Healthcare, 4D Ultrasound Facility Locator, www.gehealthcare.com/usen/ultrasound/4d/4d_sitequest_mini.html

8 Interview with Mario Cuomo broadcast on NBC, *Meet the Press,* August 7, 2005.

9 Cynthia L. Cooper, "New York Launches Probe of Crisis-Pregnancy Centers," Women's eNews, May 10, 2006, www.womensenews.org/ article.cfm/dyn/aid/801

10 Neela Banerjee, "Church Groups Turn to Sonogram to Turn Women from Abortion," *New York Times,* February 2, 2005.

11 Ibid.

12 Cited by R. Albert Mohler, "Who's Afraid of the Fetus?" *Southern Baptist Press,* February 14, 2005, www.bpnews.net/bpcolumn. asp?ID=1725

13 Sheryl Gay Stolberg, "Shifting Certainties in the Abortion War," *New York Times,* January 11, 1998.

14 Cited by Bernard Nathanson, *The Hand of God: A Journey from Death to Life by the Abortion Doctor Who Changed His Mind* (Washington, D.C.: Regnery, 1996), p. 126.

15 Ibid., p. 140.

16 Ibid., p. 126.

17 Pro-Life Action League, "Meet the Abortion Providers: Dr. Anthony Levitano," www.prolifeaction.org/providers/levitano.htm

18 Pro-Life Action League, "Meet the Abortion Providers Dr. Beverley McMillan," www.prolifeaction.org/providers/mcmillan.htm

19 Ibid.

20 Pro-Life Action League, "Meet the Abortion Providers: Joan Appleton," www.prolifeaction.org/providers/appleton.htm

21 Mary Meehan, "Ex-Abortion Workers: Why They Quit," *Human Life Review,* Spring/Summer 2000.

22 Ibid.

23 Informed Choice Act, introduced in U.S. House of Representatives, www.thomas.loc.gov/cgi-bin/query/z?c108:H.R.+195

24 Legislative Update, Informed Choice Act, Bill Summary, Susan B. Anthony List, www.sba-list.org/print.cfm?section=whatsnew&page=legupdate_informedchoice

25 Michaelene Jenkins, "Abortion: A Poor Last Resort," *San Diego Union-Tribune,* January 22, 2003.

CHAPTER 10: BACKING THE ABORTION WARS

1 Steven Ertelt, "Senator Claims 5,000 Women Will Die If Abortion Overturned," *LifeNews.com,* July 5, 2005, www.lifenews.com/nat1425.html

2 Ibid.

3 "Will Overruling *Roe* Make Abortion Illegal?" Executive Summary, Life Legal Defense Fund, July 2005, www.overruleroe.com/summary.htm

4 "What If Roe Fell? A State by State Consequence of Overturning *Roe v. Wade,*" Center for Reproductive Rights, September 2004.

5 "NARAL Falsely Accuses Supreme Court Nominee Roberts," Annenberg Political Fact Check, August 9, 2005, www.factcheck.org

6 Cited by Kathryn Jean Lopez, "Changing the Tune," *National Review Online,* August 10, 2005, www.nationalreview.com

7 Lisa Falkenberg, "AP Interview: Attorney Who Argued *Roe v. Wade* Hopes Abortion Rights March Curbs Apathy," Associated Press, April 24, 2005, www.sfgate.com/cgi-bin/article.cti?file=/news/archive/2004/04//24/national1457ED

8 Hadley Arkes, "Bush's Second Chance," *First Things,* April 2005.

9 "What If Roe Fell? State by State Consequences of Overturning *Roe v. Wade.*"

10 "An Abortion Rights Advocate Says He Lied about Procedure," *New York Times,* February 26, 1997, p. A11.

11 "Excerpts from Government's Cross-Examination of Dr. Mitchell Creinin," April 6, 2004, published in *Catalyst,* Journal of the Catholic League for Religious and Civil Rights, July/August 2004.

12 Ibid.

13 Ibid.

14 After viability, the state may "proscribe" abortion except where it is necessary, in appropriate medical judgment, for the preservation of the life or health of the mother. *Roe,* 410 U.S. at 164–165. *Doe v. Bolton,* 410 U.S. 179 (1973) defined maternal health as "all factors, physical, emotional, psychological, familial, and the woman's age— relevant to the well being of the patient."

15 The Harris Poll no. 18, March 3, 2005.

16 Zogby International Poll, April 15–17, 2004.

17 Keith L. Moore and T. V. N. Persaud, *The Developing Human: Clinically Oriented Embryology,* 7th ed. (Philadelphia: W. B. Saunders Co., 2003), p. 330.

18 Wirthlin Worldwide Poll, 2005.

19 Erika Bachiochi, *The Cost of "Choice": Women Evaluate the Impact of Abortion* (San Francisco: Encounter Books, 2004).

20 Erika Bachiochi, "The Abortion Debate," *Washington Times,* October 29, 2004.

21 Nick Cannon, "Can I Live" video, www.nickacannonmusic.com/index_main.html

22 Nick Cannon website, www.websitetoolbox.com/tool/mb/dpc123

23 Renee Graham, "Video Adds Simplistic Voice to Abortion Debate," *Tallahassee Democrat,* August 10, 2005, www.tallahassee.com

24 "Statement by U.S. Senator Barbara Boxer," press release, January 22, 2004.

25 Jeanne Cummings, "Women's Groups Prep for Court Fight," *Wall Street Journal,* August 5, 2005, p. A4.

26 Jeffrey Rosen, "Alito vs. Roberts, Word by Word," *New York Times,* January 15, 2006.

27 Byron York, "Dems Attack Alito—and Lose," *National Review Online,* January 11, 2006, www.nationalreview.com

28 David Espo, "Analysis: Abortion Key in Alito Fight," *Newsday.com,* January 12, 2006.

29 Marvin Olasky, *Abortion Rites* (Washington, D.C.: Regnery, 1995), p. 305.

30 Ibid., p. 284.

31 Ibid., p. 303.

32 Ibid., p. 304.

33 John Leland, "Some Abortion Foes Forgo Politics for Quiet Talk," *New York Times,* January 16, 2006, p. A11.

34 James Davison Hunter, *Before the Shooting Begins: Searching for Democracy in America's Culture Wars* (New York: Free Press, 1994), p. 232.

35 "Feminists for Life Redirects Grim Roe Anniversary toward Women-

Centered Activism," Feminists for Life of America, 2004, www.feministsforlife.org/news/PRRoe2006events.htm

36 Hunter, *Before the Shooting Begins,* p. 234.

INDEX

abortion clinics: "blessing" of,
89; "changing places" experiment, 147; Freedom of Access
to Clinic Entrances Act, 65,
75, 132; location of, 34,
37–38, 46; nonviolent
protests at, 67–76, 125,
136–37; RICO lawsuits, 67,
69–75, 138; sidewalk counseling at, 60, 61, 67–69, 71, 74,
114, 131, 132; violence
against, 59–66, 111; *see also*
Planned Parenthood Federation of America
Abortion Rites (Olasky), 144–45
Abramowicz v. Lefkowitz (1970),
13
Advocates for Life, 61
African Americans: abortion
rates, 31–32, 46; and AIDS,
33; clinic proximity, 34,
37–38, 46; and Clinton policies, 46; crime rates, 41–42;

and Democratic Party, 33;
"genocide" claims, 33–34;
late-term abortions, 32; in
Sanger's eugenics, 34–35, 37
AIDS, 33
Alan Guttmacher Institute, 31,
51, 55, 57, 102
Aldrich, Gillian, 80
Alito, Samuel, 5, 136, 143–44
American Association of Univer-
sity Professors, 112
American Birth Control League,
36; *see also* Planned Parent-
hood Federation of America
American Civil Liberties Union
(ACLU), 78; pro-life views in,
16
American Collegians for Life,
117
American Enterprise Institute, 42
American Institute of Ultrasound
in Medicine, 125
American Life League, 103

American Prospect Online, 122
American Psychological Association, 6
American Sociological Association, 6
Anderson, Brian C., 117
Annenberg Political Fact Check, 56, 137
Anthony, Susan B., 141
Anti-Defamation League, 66–67
Antoninus, St., 91–92
Appleton, Joan, 130–31
Aquila, Samuel (Bishop), 105
Aquinas, Thomas, St., 91, 96
Aristotle, 123
Arizona, 57, 83, 105
Arkansas, 136
Army of God, 60–64, 66, 67
Aryan Nation, 66
Asay, Chuck, 31
Associated Press, 22
Association of Catholic Colleges and Universities, 110
Augustine, St., 96
Ave Maria University, 114

Bachiochi, Erika, 141
Banerjee, Neela, 126–27
Baptist Church, 48, 86
Barrett, James H., 63
Baumgardner, Jennifer, 80
Bearing Right: How Conservatives Won the Abortion War (Saletan), 5
Before the Shooting Begins (Hunter), 61
Benedict XVI, Pope, 113
Benham, Flip, 132
Beninato, Patricia, 80
Berrigan, Daniel, 16
Biden, Joseph, 144
birth control, 4, 14, 102; and eugenics, 34–37; and race, 39–40
Birth Control Review, 35

Blackmun, Harry, 1–2
Blackmun, Sally, 1–2
Blakey, G. Robert, 69–70
Blumb, Cynthia, 89
Blumner, Robyn, 71–72
Born-Alive Infants Protection Act (2002), 138
Boston College: Reproductive Choice Coalition, 111
Boston Globe, 21, 46, 142
Boston University School of Theology, 87
Boston Women's Health Book Collective, 78
Bottcher, Rosemary, 16–17
Bourgeois, Roy (Rev.), 72
Bowie Crofton Pregnancy Center and Medical Clinic, 126–27
Boxer, Barbara, 135, 142
Bozell, Brent, 54
Bradley, Craig, 72–73
Brady, Patrick, 65
Braun, Debra, 131
breast cancer, 141
Breyer, Stephen, 73, 74–75
Brief, Liberal, Catholic Defense of Abortion, A (Dombrowski/ Deltete), 96–97
Britain, 42
Britton, John, 63
Brooks, Ann Loar, 87
Brown, John, 145
Brown, Robert, 37–38
Brown, Ron, 19
Bruskevitz, Fabian (Bishop), 105
Buffet, Warren (foundation), 28, 78
Bunning, Jim, 133
Burke, Raymond (Archbishop), 103–4, 105
Burt, John, 61
Bush, George H. W., 56
Bush, George W., 25; abortion rates under, 54–57; Supreme

Court appointments, 5, 135, 138

Caine, Michael, 81
California: assembly resolution, 83; Department of Health Services, 38–39; Medi-Cal, 39; Parents' Right to Know initiative, 138; reporting non-compliance, 32–33, 51
Call to Concern, A (1977), 57
Camasso, Michael, 52–53
"Can I Live" (song/video), 141–42
Cannon, Nick, 141–42
Cardinal Newman Society, 110, 113
Carlson, Robert (Bishop), 105
Casey, Robert, 9, 19–20
Casey, Robert, Jr., 27
Catholic Church / Catholicism, 57, 85; abortion rates in, 102–3; bishops, 48, 103–6; *Casti Connubii,* 91; Catechism of, 95–96; and Democratic Party, 11, 13–14, 17–18, 23–24; and establishment clause, 105–6; *Humanae Vitae,* 102; Immaculate Conception, 96–97; and Kennedys, 10–11, 14; Pax Christi USA, 15, 113; as "pro-choice," 90–91, 96–102; pro-choice politicians in, 103–6; Vatican U.N. status, 100–1; withholding of Communion, 103, 104–6
Catholic colleges & universities, 109–14; "evangelical pruning," 113–14; pro-choice groups at, 110–11, 113; pro-life groups at, 109, 111–12
Catholic Insight, 103
Catholics for a Free Choice, 10–11, 30, 48, 78, 95, 97–102; *Conscience* (magazine), 99; and DNC, 17–18; funding, 98, 101–2; grant distribution, 102; *New York Times* ad, 18; on Vatican status, 100–1
Catholic University of America, 113, 117
Catholic World News, 11
Center for Reproductive Rights, 136
Centers for Disease Control and Prevention (CDC), 51
Chafee, Lincoln, 27
Chaput, Charles (Archbishop), 105
Chesterton, G. K., 43
Childress, Clenard, Jr., 33–34
China: coercive abortion in, 25, 49
Choice USA, 39–40
Christ Hospital (Illinois), 138
Christian Brothers University, 113
Christian Coalition, 47
Chronicle of Higher Education, 39, 114
Cider House Rules, The (film), 81
City Journal, 117
civil-rights movement, 73
Clark, Wesley, 23–24
Clayton, Fay, 73, 74
Clinton, Bill, and administration of, 20; abortion rates under, 55–56; Freedom of Choice Act, 47; and "Gag Rule," 45–46; on Hyde amendment, 46–47; National Health Security Plan, 47–49; on partial-birth abortion, 18–19, 49; as pro-life, 15, 18; and RU-486, 49
Clinton, Hillary Rodham, 26; on abortion rates, 54, 56;

Clinton, Hillary Rodham (cont.)
National Health Security Plan,
47–49
CLOSED: 99 Ways to Stop Abortion (Scheidler), 68
Clowes, Brian, 102
Coar, David, 70
College Democrats, 118
College of the Holy Cross, 113,
114
College Republicans, 117–18
Colorado Springs Gazette Telegraph, 31
Colorado, 56, 57
Commonwealth Women's Clinic,
130
Conscience (magazine), 99
Cook, Constance, 13
Cost of "Choice," The, 141
Creinin, Mtchell, 139–40
crime rates, 40–43
crisis pregnancy centers, 116,
125–27; *New York Times* on,
145–46; opposition to,
125–27; ultrasound in,
126–28
Cuomo, Mario, 125
Curran, Charles (Fr.), 10

Daily Princetonian, 115, 118
Dartmouth Coalition for Life,
116
Daschle, Tom, 105
David Frost Show, The, 21
Davis, Angela, 112
Davis, Gray, 105
Dean, Howard, 27, 55, 56
death penalty, 104
deaths from abortion, 135–36
Dees, Morris, 111
Defensive Action, 63
DeLauro, Rosa, 106
Delaware Women's Health Organization, 69

Deltete, Robert, 96–97
Democratic Party, 9–30; and
African American churches,
33; and Alito nomination,
143–44; and Catholics,
10–11, 13–14; change of
position, 21–24; contributions to, 27–29; and
Kennedys, 9–15, 26; national
conventions, 9, 17, 18–19,
25–26; popular opinion in,
29–30; pro-life history, 15–17
Democrats for Life of America,
26–27
DePaul University, 111
DiMarzio, Nicholas (Bishop),
106
Doe v. Bolton, 136, 140
Dolan, Tim (Archbishop), 105
Dombrowski, Daniel, 96–97
Donohue, John, 40–42
Donohue, Phil, 63
Douglass, Shelley, 16
Drake, Vera, 81
Dreher, Rod, 83–84
Drinan, Robert (Fr.), 10–11, 14
Dubner, Stephen, 42

Ebert, Roger, 81
Eden Theological Seminary, 87
Edwards, John, 3–4
elections, 3–4, 5, 21, 22, 104,
106; and abortion statistics,
56–57; NARAL contributions, 27–29; and student
groups, 115
Elizabeth Cady Stanton Pregnant
and Parenting Student Services Act, 147–48
embryonic stem-cell research,
103, 105, 115
Emily's List, 27–28
Englert, Roy, 73
Episcopal Church, 84, 98

Equal Rights Amendment
    (1923), 141
eugenics, 34–37
euthanasia & assisted suicide,
    103, 105, 124
Ex Corde Ecclesiae, 112–13

FactCheck.org, 56, 137
Family Planning Advocates of
    New York State, 125–26
Farmer, Mary, 111
Feldt, Gloria, 5
Feminine Mystique, The
    (Friedan), 12
feminism, 3, 5, 10, 12, 131,
    143; pro-life, 117, 133, 141,
    146; and Sanger, 36; Women-
    Church Convergence,
    99–100
Feminist Majority, 46
Feminists for Life, 117, 133–34,
    146; College Outreach Pro-
    gram, 146
Feminist Women's Health Cen-
    ter, 81, 127
Feshkens, Edward, 48–49
Fessio, Joseph D., 114
Finkbine, Sherri, 82–83
Fitzsimmons, Ron, 139
Flynn, Ray, 26
Flynt, Larry, 110–11
Focus on the Family, 146
Fonda, Jane, 28, 29
Ford Foundation, 17, 78; and
    Catholics for a Free Choice,
    98, 101
foreign aid (abortion funding in),
    22, 23, 25, 49, 50
Foxman, Abraham, 66–67
Franciscan University, 114
Freakonomics (Levitt/Dubner),
    42–43
Frederiksen, Marilynn, 140
Freedom of Choice Act, 47

free speech rights, 5, 71, 73, 75
Friedan, Betty, 12
Friends (TV), 121
Fuchs, Joseph (Fr.), 10

Gaines, Deborah, 64–65
Gaines, Reg E., 78
Galante, Joseph (Bishop), 105
Gamble, Clarence, 35
Gandy, Kim, 73–74, 75, 110
Garrison, William Lloyd, 145
General Electric: 4D Ultrasound,
    121–22, 124–25
General Service Foundation,
    101–2
George, Francis (Cardinal), 105
George, Robert P., 122, 124
Georgetown University, 111;
    Law School, 111
Gephardt, Richard, 22–23
Gibbons, Kendyl, 90
Glamour magazine, 137
Goertzel, Ted, 53
Gonzaga University, 113
Gore, Al, 9; NARAL contribu-
    tions to, 28; pro-life history,
    15, 21–22, 47
Gorman, Michael, 87
Graduate Theological Union, 87
Graham, Renee, 142
Griffin, Michael, 60–62, 63
Grunebaum, Amos, 140
Gudorf, Christine, 91
Gunn, David, 60–62, 63, 78
Guttmacher Institute, 31, 51,
    55, 57, 102

Hafer, Barbara, 27
Hand of God, The (Nathanson),
    12
Harriman, Joan, 17
Harvard Crimson, 116
Harvard Divinity School, 87
Harvard Right to Life, 109, 116

Harvard Students for Choice, 109, 116
Hassan, Riffat, 92
Hatfield, Mark, 17
Heche, Anne, 82
Hefner, Hugh, 98
Hellwig, Monica, 110
Hentoff, Nat, 19–20
Hewlett Foundation (William & Flora), 78
Higher Education Research Institute (UCLA), 110, 118
Hill, Paul, 63, 70
Hispanic Women for Life, 38
Hitler, Adolf, 34, 36, 79
Hobbs Act, 75
Holderman, James, 69
Hollywood, 81–83
Hope Clinic for Women, 147
Houston Chronicle, 56
Hubbard, Howard, 104
Hughes, Harold, 17
Human Life International, 112
Hunter, James Davison, 5, 61, 146, 147
Hunter, Johnny (Rev.), 33
Hussey, Laura, 57
Hyde Amendment, 42

Idaho, 57
If These Walls Could Talk (film), 82
I'm Not Sorry Day, 79–81
infanticide, 122–24
Informed Choice Act (2005), 133
International Projects Assistance Services, 102
Islam, 85, 90, 92
Ivy League Coalition for Life, 116

Jackson, Jesse, 15, 16
Jacobsen, Sally, 118

Jewell, Richard, 65
John F. Kennedy Profile in Courage Award, 14
John Paul II, Pope, 112–13
Jonsen, Albert, 10
Judaism, 84, 87–88, 92–93

Keeler, William (Cardinal), 106
Kennedy, Anthony, 73
Kennedy, John F., 11–12, 13
Kennedy, Robert F., 10–11
Kennedy, Ted, 9–11, 14, 144
Kennedy Institute of Ethics, 101
Kentucky, 56
Kerry, John, 4, 24–26; on abortion rates, 54, 56; anti-Catholic positions, 103
Killea, Lucy, 18
Killing the Black Body (D. Roberts), 46
King, Larry, 24
King, Martin Luther, Jr., 37, 85–86
Kirsanov, Peter, 25
Kissling, Frances, 17–18, 98–101, 113
Kopp, James, 64
Krane, Gary, 56–57
Kucinich, Dennis, 22

"Laci and Conner's Law," 25
Lader, Larry, 12–13
Lambs of Christ, 61
Land, Richard D., 48
Langevin, James, 27
late-term abortion, 4, 9, 32, 49, 93, 104, 106; and African Americans, 32; in *Doe,* 140; opinion on, 140–41; *see also* partial-birth abortion
Latinos/Latinas, 33, 38–39, 100
Lawson, James (Rev.), 113
Leahy, Patrick, 144
Leigh, Mike, 81

Leland, John, 145–46
Leo, John, 20
Levitano, Anthony, 129–30
Levitt, Steven, 40–43
Life Education and Research
    Network (LEARN), 33
Life Legal Defense Fund, 136
Life Perspectives, 147
"live-birth abortion," 138
Loesch, Julie, 17
Louisiana, 136
Luker, Kristin, 6
Lutherans for Life, 48–49

Maguire, Daniel C., 77, 85,
    90–93, 95
Mahoney, Roger (Cardinal), 48,
    104
Manchester Union, 23–24
Mansell, Henry, 104
Marcantonio, Vito, 12
March for Women's Lives,
    39–40, 83, 85–86
Margulis, Bonnie (Rabbi), 87–88
Marie Claire magazine, 147
Marist College, 113
Martinez, Susanne, 127
Marx, Paul (Fr.), 112
Matthews, Chris, 114
McArthur, Nikki, 117
McAuliffe, Terry, 26
McCarrick, Theodore (Cardinal),
    104
McCarthy, Eugene, 16
McCormick, Richard (Fr.), 10
McCorvey, Norma, 132
McGreevey, James, 105
McMillan, Beverly, 130
McQuaid, Joseph, 23–24
McQuillan, Patricia Fogarty, 17
media, 5, 6, 13, 55, 82, 103; on
    Casey, 20; on poverty, 54;
    silence on Gore; 21; *see also*
    Hollywood

Media Research Center, 54
Medicaid, 46, 49, 52, 55, 143
Medical Students for Choice, 78
Meehan, Mary, 15, 16, 132
Meet the Press, 54–55, 56
Melendez, Marcella, 38
Mellman, Mark, 28
Mengeling, Carl, 104
Methodist Church, 84
Michaels, George, 13–14
Michelman, Kate, 22, 27, 110;
    on Clinton policies, 46
Michigan, 56, 57, 136
Milhaven, Giles (Fr.), 10–11
military hospitals, 49, 50, 143
Miller, Michael, 113
minors & parental involvement,
    4, 9, 25, 26, 59, 138
MIT Pro-Life, 109, 115–16
*Mix My Blood with the Blood of the
    Unborn* (Hill), 63
Montoya-Humphrey, Colette
    Denali, 39–40
Moody, Harold, 13
Moore, Demi, 82
Mosher, Stephen, 37
Mostre, Kim, 103
MoveOn.org, 143
Ms. Magazine, 78
Mulcahay, Meta, 17
Murray, Charles, 42
Murray, John Courtney (Fr.), 10
Myers, John (Bishop), 105

Napolitano, Janet, 105
NARAL Pro-Choice America,
    12, 48, 110; and Clinton poli-
    cies, 46; and crisis pregnancy
    center "sting," 126; Demo-
    cratic contributions, 27–29;
    on Gephardt, 22–23; on
    Kerry, 24; on Kucinich, 22;
    PAC, 28–29; on Roberts &
    Alito, 136–37, 143

NAS (rap artist), 141

Nathanson, Bernard, 12–13; on abortion death statistics, 135; change of heart, 128–29; quoted, 3; *Silent Scream*, 131*n*

National Abortion and Reproduction Rights Action League (NARAL), 28

National Abortion Federation, 65, 89, 98

National Abortion Rights Action League (NARAL), 12, 19, 78, 128; *see also* NARAL Pro-Choice America

National Association for Repeal of Abortion Laws (NARAL), 12

National Baptist Convention, 86

National Center for Health Statistics, 135

National Coalition of Abortion Providers, 139

National Conference of Catholic Bishops, 48

National Day of Appreciation for Abortion Providers, 77–79

National Network of Abortion Funds, 80

National Organization for Women, 17, 18, 78, 111, 130; decline in donations, 143; RICO lawsuits by, 67–76

National Pro-Life March, 116

National Right to Life Committee, 22

Nazareth College, 111

Nazis, 36

Neu, Diann, 89

New England Journal of Medicine, 128–29

New Jersey, 52–54

Newsweek, 60

New York State, 13–14, 98

New York Times, 27, 28, 61; on Alito, 143; on Clinton policies, 46; on crisis pregnancy centers, 145–46; Kissling ad, 99; on ultrasound, 126–27

Nietzsche, Friedrich, 34, 36

Nisbet, Matthew, 122

Noonan, Peggy, 29

Northern Kentucky University, 118

Norton, Eleanor Holmes, 113

NOW v. Scheidler, 67–76; as class-action suit, 70–71; dismissal, 69; "pattern of violence" argument, 70; and pro-life donations, 71; and RICO, 67, 69–74; strange bedfellows, 72; Supreme Court rulings, 74–76; Terry settlement, 70; as vendetta, 72

O'Bannon, Randy, 57

O'Connor, Sandra Day, 3

Oklahoma, 136

Olasky, Marvin, 124, 144–45

O'Leary, Brad (O'Leary Report), 29–30

Olmstead, Thomas (Bishop), 105

Olson, Ted, 73

O'Malley, Sean (Archbishop), 105

Operation Rescue, 69, 70

Operation See Change, 100–1

opinion polls, 25–26, 29–30, 59; on partial-birth abortion, 140–41; on taxpayer funding, 47, 59

Packard Foundation (David & Lucile), 28, 78, 98

Padovano, Anthony, 97

Palumbo, Pam, 127

parental notification, 4, 9, 25, 26, 59, 138

partial-birth abortion, 4, 22; Clinton on, 18–19, 49; Congress on, 138–39; description, 139–40; frequency, 139; Kerry on, 25; public opinion on, 25–26, 139, 140–41; state bans, 139

Paul, Alice, 141

Pax Christi USA, 15, 113

Pearl, Karen, 28

Pensacola Ladies Center, 69

People for the American Way, 143

People for the Ethical Treatment of Animals (PETA), 72–73

Pennsylvania, 56

Perry, Michael, 36

Petersen, Laci & Conner, 25

Pius IX, Pope, 96–97

Pius XI, Pope, 91

Pivot of Civilization, The (Sanger), 34, 35–36, 40

Planned Parenthood Federation of America, 5, 67; and Catholic colleges, 110, 111, 113; and celebration, 78, 79; clinics, 126, 132; on Clinton health plan, 48; and Democratic Party, 23–24, 27–28; facility blessing, 89; and Guttmacher Institute, 55; and minority communities, 34; protests at, 68; and Roberts nomination, 143; and Sanger, 34, 36–37; and sidewalk counselors, 132

Plato, 123

Playboy Foundation, 98

Politics of Motherhood, The (Luker), 6

Pollitt, Katha, 80

Ponnuru, Ramesh, 42

Population Research Institute, 37

Prejean, Helen (Sister), 72

Presbyterian Church, 84

Pre-Term Health Services, 64–65

Princeton Pro-Life, 115, 118

Princeton Theological Seminary, 87

Prisoners of Christ website, 62

Private Matter, A (film), 82–83

Pro-Choice America. *See* NARAL Pro-Choice America

Pro-Choice Vote, 29

Profile in Courage Award, 14

Progressive, The, 15

Pro-Life Action League, 67–75; nonviolent mission, 67–68

Pro-Life Action Ministries, 131

Pro-Lifers for Survival, 17

Providence College, 113–14

public funding (of abortion), 18, 22, 25; in Clinton administration, 45–50; and Hyde amendment, 42, 46–47; and "Gag Rule," 45; public opinion on, 47, 59; and race, 38–39; and undocumented aliens, 39; and welfare reform, 50–54

Public Health Service Act: Title X, 45

public schools, 25

Quinn, Michael, 32

Ragsdale, Katherine Hancock (Rev.), 85–86, 89

Reagan, Ronald, 68, 137

Refuse and Resist, 78–79

Reid, Harry, 26

Reilly, Daniel (Bishop), 114

religion, 4, 48, 85–93; "celebrating" abortion, 77, 83–84; and "holy" choice, 85, 87–90; Islam, 85, 90, 92; Judaism, 84, 87–88, 92–93; liberal

religion (cont.)
churches, 10; Seminarians for Choice, 87; Unitarians, 83–84, 86, 90; *see also* Catholic Church/Catholicism

Religious Coalition for Reproductive Choice (RCRC), 77, 84, 85–89; civil-rights theme, 85–86; *Faith and Choice* (newsletter), 86; mission statement, 86; *Prayerfully Pro-Choice,* 88–89; seminary course, 86–87

Republican Party, 17; in colleges, 117–18; popular opinion in, 29–30; pro-choice politicians in, 27*n*

Rhode Island, 136

RICO Act, 67, 69–74

Risen, James, 60

risks of abortion, 32, 141

Roberts, Dorothy, 46

Roberts, John, 5, 135; attack ads on, 136–37, 143

Rockefeller, Nelson, 13

Rodriguez, Jordan, 117

Roe v. Wade, 1–3, 5, 15, 135–36, 142–43; anniversary celebrations, 23, 45, 80, 83–84, 87–88, 127; Blackmun's motives, 1–2; and *Call to Concern,* 57; and crime rates, 41; and Freedom of Choice Act, 47; Gore on, 21, 22; as "inevitable," 3; legal criticism of, 2; McCorvey's change on, 132; public opinion on, 140–41; and state law, 136; *Webster* challenge, 6

Roemer, Tim, 26–27

Roman Catholic Church. *See* Catholic Church Catholicism

Rossi, Peter, 53

Rounds, Mike, 138

RU-486 ("morning-after pill"), 49, 111

Rudolph, Eric Robert, 65–66

Ruether, Rosemary, 99–100

Russert, Tim, 54, 56

Russia, 42

Sacred Choices (Maguire), 85, 90–93

Saletan, William, 5

Salvi, John, 64

same-sex marriage, 103, 105, 110

San Diego News Notes, 39

San Diego Union-Tribune, 18

Sanger, Margaret, 12, 40; on charity, 35; eugenics, 34–37; "Maggie Award," 37

Santa Clara University, 111

Santorum, Rick, 27*n*, 101

Scalia, Antonin, 73

Scheidler, Joseph, 67–76, 78

Schlossberg, Caroline Kennedy, 9

Schneider, Laurel, 87

Schumer, Charles E., 27, 144

Schussler-Fiorenza, Elizabeth, 99–100

Seamless Garment Network, 72

Seattle University, 111

See Change Campaign, 100–1

Seminarians for Choice, 87

Shannon, James Patrick, 102

Shannon, Rachelle, 61–63, 70

Sharpton, Al, 24

Sheridan, Michael (Bishop), 105

Shields, Mark, 26

Siegan, Bernard, 2

Silent Scream (film), 131

Singer, Peter, 123–24

slavery, 4, 104, 115; abolitionists, 145

Slepian, Barnett, 64

Smeal, Eleanor, 46, 69
Smith, Bob, 101
Smith, Christopher H., 52, 101
Smith, JoAnn, 126
Smith, John (Bishop), 105
Smith, Philip (Rev.), 114
Social Darwinism, 36
social sciences, 6
Sofer, Moses (Rabbi), 87
Sojourners magazine, 16
sonograms. *See* ultrasound
Soros, George, 28
South Dakota, 57, 136, 138
Southern Baptist Convention, 48
Southern Christian Leadership
    Conference, 72
Southern Poverty Law Center,
    61, 111
Spacek, Sissy, 82–83
Spitzer, Eliot, 113, 125–26
St. Antoninus Institute for
    Catholic Education in Busi-
    ness, 91–92
Stanek, Jill, 138
Stanford Students for Life, 109
Stanton, Elizabeth Cady, 141,
    147
Stassen, Glen Harold, 56–57
state law, 3, 5, 40–41, 136; Ari-
    zona, 83, 105; California,
    138; New York, 13–14, 98;
    partial-birth abortion bans,
    139; South Dakota, 57, 136,
    138
Staunton, Imelda, 81
Stearns, Cliff, 133
Steinem, Gloria, 113
Stephanopoulos, George, 46
Stoddard, Lothrop, 35
student groups: American Colle-
    gians for Life, 117; College
    Democrats, 118; College
    Republicans, 117–18; Medical
    Students for Choice, 78; pro-

choice, 109–11, 116; pro-life,
    111–12, 114–19; Seminarians
    for Choice, 87
suicide, 141
Summa theologica (Aquinas), 96
Supreme Court of the United
    States. *See* United States
    Supreme Court
Sykes, Jay, 16

Taylor, Kathy, 19
Terry, Randall, 69, 70
Texas Department of Health, 37
thalidomide, 83
Thomas, Judy, 60
Thomas Aquinas, St., 91, 96
Thomas More Society Pro-Life
    Law Center, 73
Tiller, George, 61, 62
Tiller, Robert (Rev.), 87
Tocqueville, Alexis de, 146
Trinity College, 113
Turley, Jonathan, 72
Turner, Ted, 28; Turner Founda-
    tion, 29, 78, 98

Ullman, Emily, 14
ultrasound imaging, 121–22;
    abortionist response to,
    128–32; GE ad, 121–22,
    124–25; and Informed
    Choice Act, 132–33; opposi-
    tion to, 124–26; *Silent
    Scream*, 131*n;* women's
    response to, 122, 124–25,
    126–28
Unborn Child Pain Awareness
    Act, 138
Unborn Victims of Violence Act
    ("Laci and Conner's Law"),
    25, 138
Union Theological Seminary, 87
Unitarian Universalist Associa-
    tion/Church, 83–84, 86, 90

United Church of Christ, 84, 89
United Methodist Church, 84
United Nations, 98; Family Planning Administration, 49; Population Fund, 25; Vatican status, 100–1
United States Census Bureau, 39
United States Congress: Black Caucus, 18; Born-Alive Infants Protection Act, 138; Elizabeth Cady Stanton Pregnant and Parenting Student Services Act, 147–48; Freedom of Choice Act, 142–43; and Hyde amendment, 46, 47; Informed Choice Act, 133; on partial-birth abortion, 138–39; Unborn Child Pain Awareness Act, 138; Unborn Victims of Violence Act, 138; welfare reform, 50–52, 54
United States Constitution: First Amendment, 5, 71, 73, 75; Fourteenth Amendment, 2
United States Court of Appeals, Seventh Circuit, 69, 71
United States Supreme Court: Alito nomination, 5, 136, 143–44; *Doe v. Bolton,* 136, 140; *NOW v. Scheidler,* 69–70, 72–76, 138; Roberts nomination, 5, 135, 136–37, 143; *Webster v. Reproductive Health Services,* 6; *see also Roe v. Wade*
United Theological Seminary, 87
University of Pennsylvania Students for Life, 109
University of San Diego, 111–12
U.S. Conference of Catholic Bishops, 106

U.S. News & World Report, 20, 47

Vatican: U.N. status, 100–1
Vatican Congregation for Catholic Education, 113
Veazey, Carlton W. (Rev.), 84, 86
Vera Drake (film), 81
Vieques Support Committee, 72
Villanova University, 111
violence, 59–66; clinic bombing, 60, 62, 63, 65–66, 67; shooting, 60–65, 70
Voices in the Wilderness, 72

Wall Street Journal, 37, 42, 143
War Choice, The (Feldt), 5
Washington Post, 24, 46, 47; *Magazine,* 98
Webster v. Reproductive Health Services, 6
Weddington, Sarah, 137
Weigand, William (Bishop), 105
Weigel, George, 112
welfare, 50–54; family cap, 51–54, 133, 146; "illegitimacy bonus," 50–51, 54
Wenski, Thomas (Bishop), 105
Western Washington University, 119
White, Byron, 2
White, Karen, 27
Wisconsin, 57, 136
Wollstonecraft, Mary, 141
Woman and the New Race (Sanger), 34
Woman's Choice, A, 146
Women-Church Convergence, 99–100
Wooden, Frederick, 83
WORLD magazine, 124

Writings on an Ethical Life (Singer), 123

Yard, Molly, 131

Zogby, John (poll), 29–30
Zoloth, Laurie, 92–93